Emerge

Real Stories of Courage and Truth

Cassandra Washington
& One Degree Shift

Emerge

Front Cover Design: Alicia White
Back Cover Design: MJ Schwader
Interior Design and Layout: MJ Schwader
Editor: MJ Schwader

ISBN-13: 978-1517256906
ISBN-10: 1517256909

Table of Contents

Dedication

I dedicate this book to my "Uncle," Ervin Price Jr. He gave me the gift and awesome privilege of coauthoring his last chapter on this side of Heaven. I will always remember your cheerful smile and the little dance you did when you were happy. I am thankful for the time we shared. Rest in peace.

Emerge

Acknowledgments

"Alone we can do so little;
together we can do so much."
– Helen Keller

A special thanks to my mom who maintained my house and saw to me taking care of myself as we completed this book.

Thank you One Degree Shift community and my awesome co-authors: Patricia Alston-Rochon, Darcie Beyer, Sandra Brooks, Precilla Feliciano Calara, Elizabeth Corbell, Susan W. Corbran, Anita Boutwell-Dixon, Suzanne R. Duque, Johnnene Gay, Ilda Grimaldo, Maria "MJ" Martinez, Allison McFadden, Michelle J. Perzan, Johanna Rochon, Kali Rodriguez, Gillian Smith, and Diana Towsley. I am sincerely grateful for your confidence and trust in my leadership and your willingness to go deep!

Thank you to MJ Schwader, writing coach extraordinaire! I am honored to serve alongside you in this program. I learn from you each time we talk.

Thank you to Alicia White, incredible graphic artist and mind-reader! Our cover design is breathtaking.

Thank you to my friends and colleagues who never grew weary as I read stories aloud, providing feedback on everything from phrasing and color to book title options and book description. My heart is gladdened by the abundance of support that is always here for me.

Thank you God, Heavenly Father and Soon-coming King – the source of my inspiration.

Emerge

Foreword

**"There is a butterfly in each of us waiting to emerge.
But often the old must dissolve before we discover
our wings." – Jane Lee Logan**

Welcome to the journey! My One Degree Shift community and I have been expecting you. This is the second in a series of inspirational books. In our first book, *Strengthen Your Wings*, we shared amazing stories of determination, courage, and hope – experiences that strengthened our confidence and our attitude toward success. In this book, we write of turning points in life where we made critical choices that changed our story, changed our perception, or changed our life – and that made all the difference.

Each of us has a story – a way of perceiving an event happening around us. Although our experiences may differ, there is one thing that stays true for all of us: The way we see our stories will either empower us forward, allowing us to fly, or stifle our evolution, causing us to stumble beneath our true potential.

Consider this folk tale, which originated in India, of the blind men and the elephant:

Four blind men were sharing their ideas about what they thought the elephant was like. One of the blind men was touching the elephant's tail and said, "The elephant is like a rope." Another touching the elephant's leg said, "No, an elephant is not like a rope; an elephant is like a tree trunk." The one touching the elephant's side belly said, "No an elephant is not like a rope or a tree trunk; an elephant is like a wall." The other, touching the elephant's trunk, said, "No, not like a wall, not like a tree trunk, not like a rope; it's a hose. An elephant is like a big hose." Every one of these men was accurate, according to their own perspective, yet they were blinded to the whole picture because they were only touching a portion of the elephant.

Our perspective is the selective lens by which we view the world. We see what we accept as true, yet we are often unaware of how our belief is contributing to the outcomes of our lives. The way we choose to describe an event can either perpetuate a negative experience or give way to a powerful lesson to share with all of us.

There are critical times in our lives when we get a glimpse of who we are being. We see ourselves through the decisions we make, through our repeated behaviors, or through a life-changing experience. It is in those times that life offers us a gift – a choice to shrink or shine. Difficult experiences in life often offer us the most profound reflection.

Like the blind men, we frequently only see part of our story. Shifting our perspective allows us to break free from our self-imposed limitations by seeing our life experiences as part of our development. Then we will emerge from who we've known ourselves to be and recognize who we really are. This transformation is about self-acceptance, dissolving the old perception of self and giving you permission to fly. In doing so, you'll stand in the truth of your story in a way that empowers you while encouraging others to do the same.

In this book, we share the messages found through the events of our lives to help you shift your perspective and find your wings. Using experience as the teacher, we're retelling the stories that have shaped us.

Through writing, my co-authors and I have uncovered the profound lessons found in our stories, and in the process we were transformed, because as you change the way you see your story, you will also change the way you see yourself. The process of completing this book was more than a simple writing exercise; it was an opportunity to grow personally by conquering the fears that keep us from standing in our authentic power and beauty.

I witnessed my coauthors navigate the winding roads of the journey as they bravely opened their hearts to lead the way for every reader traveling with us. Along the way, I saw their hearts expand to return to themselves the same compassion often given freely to others. I had the privilege of leading my coauthors as they faced the turbulence of their fears, uncovered the vulnerabilities of their experiences, and mined the triumphant lessons that were there for all of us to soar. They chose to remain coachable through the process, strengthening their wings along the way. Each author chose attitudes of faith and persistence as they relived a buried past or stepped into an uncertain future. During the writing process, we were encouraged by the camaraderie of community and held safely in its arms as we experienced our own transformation. A conversion that allowed us to stand in the truth of who we are today and the hope that we endeavor to become. Community was the supportive cocoon that allowed us to become chapters in each other's lives as we discovered our wings.

Are you a Difference Maker? We invite you to join us as we continue our journey together. Learn more about this thriving community at www.onedegreeshift.com.

Emerge

Stepping Out of My Story

By Cassandra Washington

"Fear, to a great extent, is born of a story we tell
ourselves, and so I chose to tell myself
a different story." — Cheryl Strayed

I sat on the edge of my seat in a meeting room packed with 500 other people. As I took notes and listened to every instruction that came from the speaker at the front of the room, I assured myself that surely this was the place where I would find the roadmap to success in my business.

Trainers are some of the worst students in the classroom, and I'm no exception. It's difficult to stay engaged because I'm constantly thinking of different ways to convey the information being presented. Throughout the presentation I was thinking, *Oh, I like how she illustrated that point. I can't wait to share it with others* or a hundred other similar thoughts. I had to continuously remind myself to *take off your teacher hat and put on your learner hat*. For the most part I was able to do that.

Then the speaker asked a provoking question: "What is the story you're telling yourself that is holding you back?" *That's an interesting question*, I thought to myself. And immediately I had my teacher hat on again. I told myself, *I'm not telling myself any story. I speak to myself in a positive way. I don't know what she is talking about.*

Then my inner coach voice reminded me of my intention for being there and said, *Drop your teacher persona; be the student.* In the last few seconds of the reflection time, it came to me that I often say to myself that things are hard and I can't depend on anyone else to help me. *Could that be the story that's holding me back?*

There wasn't enough time to ponder it for long because the speaker was on to the next part of the exercise. This time she posed a new question, equally perplexing: "What event happened that caused you to write that story?" Again I contemplated the question a bit, searching for the answer. *I don't know what she's talking about. I didn't write this story. It is not make-believe. This is a true story. I do have to work hard. For 10 years in my business, I've tried hard to do what I feel called to do and I often struggle because the revenue just doesn't flow the way I need it to at times. And, there is no one around to help me. Who can I ask for help? It's only me!*

Then my inner coach nudged me again to play along as a learner. At the time, I was clueless. *I have no idea what happened to cause me to write such a story.* Then the speaker asked us to share our discovery with a partner. *Oh, great!* I said in my sarcastic inside voice. Then my coach kicked in. *Maybe you can learn something from hearing what your partner came up with.* So I asked her to go first.

I was amazed at how easily she identified stories (plural, more than one) – the inside dialogue she had with herself that was crippling her efforts to move forward. She knew exactly which incidents in her life created them. *Was I so stuck in my teacher mode that I was unable to gain that kind of awareness about my own situation?*

Somewhat reluctantly, I shared the little insight I had gotten. "Well," I told my partner, "I often say that I have to work hard for everything I get and nothing comes easy for me. I guess that's my story, but I haven't pinpointed exactly where it came from..." Then I rationalized in my mind, *...because it is true, not a story. It's always been the case for as long as I care to remember. The story is so much a part of me that once while attending an event, a friend expectantly declared that she would win one of the door prizes, but I was convinced, "Not me. Nothing ever comes that easy for me."*

The speaker then explained that the story you tell yourself keeps you playing small and holds you back from achieving more. *Could she be right? Was this story holding me back?* I couldn't see it then, but I desperately wanted to rid myself of any belief that may be keeping me from experiencing more fulfillment and purpose. *What do I have to do to change it?*

It felt like the speaker had read my mind and was talking directly to me because in the next moment, she told us: "You can't change the event that created the story, but you can change what you tell yourself about it." She instructed us to create a new mantra that counteracted the first one. So, if my story was I had to work hard and nothing came easy for me, I certainly wanted to stop creating that reality. My thought was, *Doing what you love shouldn't be hard; it should be easy. If you love what you do, you'll likely do more of it, and in doing so, you'll get pretty good at it, and because you're good at it, it will be easy.*

I was certainly tired of everything being so hard! So I quickly created a new mantra and wrote it down: "Things come to me with ease." But I didn't stop there; I wanted to rewrite the rest of my story, specifically the part about doing it alone.

The dream I had in my heart, the purpose I felt called to fulfill, wasn't something I could do on my own. I needed support. The problem was I didn't trust people to help me. People, I learned growing up, will let you down. Even God would let you down. I didn't want to be disappointed anymore. So rather than be hurt by others, I'd better do it myself.

And then a question seared in my thoughts: *Who hurt me? Could this be the event the speaker was alluding to?*

It wasn't until after the conference, several weeks later, that the event that created my story was revealed. It was my father who hurt me. After my parents divorced, whenever I needed money for school activities and asked him for help, he either refused me – which let me down – or I had to beg him for help, which was dreadfully humiliating. He made something that should have been simple and easy so difficult for me. So I took that to mean: "I have to work hard for everything, and nothing comes easy for me." Didn't I tell you it was a true story?

My realization went even further than my dealings with my father. Perhaps the biggest letdown was an incident I wrote about in our first book, *Strengthen Your Wings*, when my cousin, my best friend, died in a tragic car accident when I was young. When I got the news of his passing, I begged, pleaded, cried, and shouted to demonstrate my deep sorrow to God. I was certain that God would see how grieved I was with my cousin's untimely death and bring him back to me. But that didn't happen. At the time, I concluded that it was a waste of time to show such remorse, so I toughened up and carried on. Not only did I disown my tears, I also abandoned my vulnerability. I unconsciously vowed that I would never be put in a position of powerlessness again. I must always be in control of everything concerning me. And that's exactly what showed up in my life.

As I sat in my seat at the conference I realized that I didn't want "hard" anymore, and I started to believe what the speaker told us, that I have the power to rewrite my story and create a different reality. So I ended my new mantra with support: "Things come to me with ease and through my trusted friends." I realized that I did have supportive people in my life that I could trust, and I have the ability to attract even more trusted friends to me.

During the conference, I physically mourned the loss of my limiting story; a flood of healing tears burst the dams of my soul. Crying, especially in public, is an emotion I forsook long ago, but that weekend I found myself crying at the least of moments. I was like a sponge drenched with water, pouring out with the slightest squeeze. I cried for weeks following the conference. I didn't understand why, but I could not hold back the tears. I believe it symbolized a collapse of the walls I constructed to keep my heart safe, to keep me certain, to help me avoid disappointment, hurt, and helplessness. Not only did the old story no longer serve me moving forward, it held me back from experiencing the fullness of life that I yearned for inside. The story had become my identity and a measure of who I could be in the world. The story imprisoned me behind walls of shame, mistrust, and struggle.

To say that uncovering the story and seeing it for its falsehood was a turning point in my life is an understatement. This new awareness was the start of something wonderful unfolding. I was returning to who I really am, rediscovering myself, and becoming the leader I was born to be.

If I am not that story, then who am I? If life is not hard then what is it? If I can trust myself, others, God, then what is possible now? If I have the power to change my story, then what can I create and who will stop me?

I began to emerge as the empowered creator that I was destined to be. This truth is not only for me. It is for everyone. We have all created stories to protect us from our deepest hurts. Stories we wrote long ago, and then recreated them in our lives over and over again until they were stuck in our psyche, permanent pillars that enclosed us behind gates of captivity. The stories were often created out of life events, some traumatic. Although those experiences were never intended to define us, the stories we wrote about them became ways in which we expressed our fears and dis-ease.

The stories we tell ourselves influence how we show up in the world because they become the lens by which we perceive and engage with life. Our experiences were meant to be teachers, and not guardians of our soul. We were not meant to be prisoners to our stories, but students of these life lessons in order to guide and transform the souls of others. Instead, our stories often hold us captive and even less attentive to the needs we are called to fulfill in the world.

So my new mantra, "Life is easy and support is always ever-present," is the reality that I live now. Unlocking the shackles of ineptness and opening the door to abundant sufficiency, my thoughts, stories, actions, and beliefs continue to open to the unlimited nature of life, of God, of love, of me, and of you.

When did I emerge? When I recognized my limiting story and chose to step out of it. This simple shift in perspective gave me the ability to see the necessity of standing in my truth. There were other things I learned as well: That my pain is not a deterrent, but a powerful teacher. Loss is not a penalty, but an invitation to open to more. Fear is not an enemy, but a staunch ally to the truth hidden inside.

Many fail to peer behind the darkness of their story to behold the beauty and truth that awaits them. The authors of this book have done that. Each searched for and found the other side of the story; the part of the story that empowers, that yields the light of who they are or who they were or who they have yet to become. As each one of them turned to the truth hidden deep within, they found wisdom, they found healing, they found the love that was there all along, calling out to them to seek it. The heart of each author has opened, inviting you to see her story as a reflection back to you. Perhaps we are called to go first, as leaders, in our journey to transform and emerge with wings of strength; a strength that we did not know we had, only discovering that truth now as we breathe out the past and enter the newness of the future.

Finding My Roux

By Johanna Rochon

"And the day came where the risk to remain in a tight bud became more painful than the risk it took to blossom." – Anais Nin

As I look in the mirror I see remnants of her face in mine. When I speak I hear myself saying similar phrases she would say. Her hurts and fears are also within me. Since I was little I could sense that something weighed heavily on her spirit. It wasn't until this very book was in the midst of being written, when my mother also became a contributing author, that I became aware that she was a victim of a traumatic sexual assault. Knowing this triggered an awakening within me. I was proud of her for having the voice to share a burden that she held on to, unspoken of for so many years. For so long she operated as normal, while being uncared for, yet finally the caged bird can sing. As it sings it sounds beautiful. It is through her transformation that I have had the courage and strength to undergo a transformation of my own.

"It all begins with the roux" is a mantra that I've repeated for the past few years. It means that you need to have a good solid foundation before you can do anything else. When making gumbo, your roux has to be perfected before you can even think about adding crabs, shrimp, sausage, or any other seasonings that make even the most conservative of people reach for a second, or even a third serving. In essence, your roux is who you are at the core, all your passions, gifts, and talents forming together to make an unduplicated you. Although I had dubbed this saying, I was never quite tested with the meaning of it until a few months ago when I had to indeed find my own roux.

"Girl you've got a good job, don't leave that!"

"What if you can't find another job, then what are you going to do?"

These are just two of the comments I heard from people when I was faced with the decision of furthering my career at the only company I had been with since I had graduated college or to spread my wings and try something else. My company was moving from one area of the city to another and employees were given the decision to stay or to separate from the company.

Day in and day out I struggled with what I should do. One minute I made up my mind to stay and literally a minute later I was thinking it would be better to try something new. I was an emotional rollercoaster riding the peaks and valleys of indecisiveness. I didn't know what to do! I was constantly looking to everyone else for the answer to my first major "adult decision".

"Could someone just tell me what to do?" I wanted this to go away, I wanted to stop spending every waking second thinking about my life path. If I made the wrong decision I would be filled with regret. But not making a decision caused so much anxiety.

This taxed heavily on me as the days passed and I was nearing the deadline of making a decision. At the 11th hour, with sweat beads running from my forehead, I still felt as torn as I did in the first hour. *I'll just stay; play it safe*, I told myself as I electronically cast a vote of "Yes".

After a few days passed, I didn't feel proud about the decision I had made. Something was eating at me and urging me to undo my decision. *If you change your mind you will look crazy*, I thought. *I'll just keep moving along with where my life is taking me*, is what my internal doubter voice once again persuaded me to do.

Then one day while I was driving along the curves and barren scenery of I-20, India Arie's chorus "running round in circles, lost my focus, lost sight of my goals" escaped from the speakers of my stereo. I had listened to that song "Little Things" so many times, but it was as if it was the first time because those words had never resonated with me in that way before.

As her lyrics seeped through my mind and made their way to my heart, it was as if the song was composed just for me. I needed to hear that message. It made me think that in life you have to make decisions for you, not what other people think. You have to be true to yourself, true to your roux.

Had I been being true to mine?

I knew deep down that I had not. I envisioned myself older, trapped in a job and unhappy, all because I didn't take a risk due to being so pre-occupied with other people's thoughts and opinions. That feeling made me shudder.

Finally, I thought about my mother and the stance she had taken by writing her story. She was brave enough to share with the world her burdens and fears, and be renewed from it. She spoke up and let go of any preconceived notions of what others would think. I wanted that same energy to exude from me.

I have a voice in this, is what I told myself, *it needs to be heard*. All my life I had played it safe, gone with the flow; it was time to leave the cocoon of warmth and comfort and emerge into a new environment. I had been provided with all the spiritual guidance, love, and words of wisdom needed to embark upon a transformational journey. There was only one thing left to do: Fly.

With a confidence I hadn't possessed before, I revoked my original decision. I decided that I did not want to transfer my employment. People's opinions and thoughts all flew out my car window, along with all the dust mites that had gathered in the air. As I exited the interstate, what remained was my roux.

I am starting anew. I plan to fulfill the things I have a passion for, such as writing, entrepreneurial ventures, and mentoring others. I am removing all the static and clutter that surround me, while chasing my wildest dreams.

It all begins with the roux, and I am on the journey to perfect mine.

Acknowledgments

To my mother, I am so proud of you for sharing your truth; you continue to be an inspiration to me daily. Thank you to My Love, friends, family, and co-workers that supported me in this journey. I am so thankful for God's gift, the blessing that enabled me to tell my story. I appreciate this group's help and advice that refined it.

Write Your Own Script

By Anita Boutwell-Dixon

"Death and life are in the power of the tongue; they that love it shall eat the fruit thereof." – Proverbs 18:21

While attending an on-the-job training session, I was captivated by the energy, enthusiasm, and excitement that emanated from one presenter in particular. It was obvious that she enjoyed her work and did it effortlessly.

After the presentation, I noticed the presenter seated in the lounge area. It was the perfect opportunity to dialogue. I eagerly asked, "Cassandra, how can I do what you do, and get paid for it?" To be honest, I don't even remember the response. All I know is that something inside was saying, "There must be more to my existence than playing a role in a job that is somewhat unfulfilling. This script no longer works for me." A fire ignited in my soul to live a life of greatness with zest, passion, and excitement.

She asked about my gifts and what I enjoyed doing outside of work. I shared that I am a minister of the Gospel. I am confident with public speaking and could easily transfer those skills into doing what she does for a living – motivating people to change. Using my God-given talents to inspire employees in the workplace would be the best of both worlds. I also told Cassandra of my love for writing and that I had been honing that gift since I was a young girl. In addition to all of that, I shared that I occasionally entertained thoughts of starting my own company.

We exchanged business cards and promised to keep in touch. Little did I know, my life had taken an invisible turn. God was setting the stage for a new act that would drastically transform me.

Almost a year later I heard from Cassandra. She gave me the fabulous invitation to be a contributing author in the very book that you are reading! I leaped at the opportunity to become a published author, a lifelong dream. What I wasn't expecting was that the preparatory writing assignments would force me to look deep inside my soul for issues that I needed to confront with truth before I would be able to share my message with others.

In the meantime, I was moved to another department at work. My responsibilities changed immensely, and projects that I deemed rewarding were taken away. I was even assigned duties for which I received zero training. The only way I completed them was by praying to God for instruction, grace, and wisdom.

Shockingly, I was put on a performance improvement plan two months later. I was infuriated and felt like I'd been set up for failure. As a godly woman, I believe in completing my work in the spirit of excellence because I have to answer to a higher power. Did I make mistakes? Yes, of course. All humans do. This is what helps us to grow and mature. It crowns us with wisdom that cannot be obtained any other way.

I was constantly told that I was performing below my job level, even though other managers I supported were pleased with my work. This boss tried to find errors in everything I did, constantly telling me who I was not – while I reminded myself of who God says I am. Once, I was asked to schedule 35 meetings, then scolded like a misbehaving child because I forgot to invite someone to one of them.

The job was not only chaotic, but became mentally draining, then downright exhausting. There is nothing more horrible than waking up, dragging yourself out of bed, and driving to a job that no longer serves a purpose – except for a paycheck to meet life's basic needs. I arrived faithfully every day expecting to be examined under the "mistake microscope". It was like serving the boss from Hell. She was the catalyst that pushed me out of my comfortable eagle's nest to soar into my life's purpose. It was a stressful and tumultuous journey, but God would make everything work in my favor.

All of my life I was programmed to jump into a mold that every generation before me aspired to fit. It goes like this – get an education, get a job, always save money for a rainy day, work over 60 years for a paycheck. If you're lucky you'll make it to retirement. Then you can really enjoy life.

Are you kidding me?

Then I recalled that Cassandra was fulfilling her purpose. I wanted that same thing for myself.

Being part of this writing project really put me in touch with my authentic self, the person that God created me to be. I realized that I was now on the precise path of destiny, while in a bloody conflict with the forces of darkness. I began to feel like a square peg being forced into a round hole. There was nothing wrong with me, only my perspective.

That changed rapidly as I accepted that I was being called to something greater – fulfilling the purpose for which I was created. It was time to stop toiling and striving in a place of chaos, and walk into God's peace. Time to break out of the cookie cutter mold that was suffocating my potential and stifling my creativity. It was time to be unleashed into endless possibilities; time to unlock the greatness inside of me.

My moment of truth had arrived. I walked into the boss's office and took control of my life. I conveyed that the unwarranted plan wasn't working for me, the job was no longer rewarding, and I refused to regress in my career. I informed her that I had already starting planning a future outside of the company. It was time to maximize my potential and use my talents in a place where they will be appreciated. I have more to offer the world. There are treasures inside of me yet to be unearthed. With joyful glee, I announced my plans to leave the company.

I was ready to put the pedal to the metal, let the rubber burn the pavement as I drove off, and never look back – except to tell my story. Not only can you change the script for your life, you can completely rewrite it! It just takes a one degree shift in your perspective of life. I have changed the course of my destiny through my words. I live by Proverbs 18:21. The words that I speak are what God says about me. I believe only that, and expect to see the fulfillment of His word in my life. I am reaping a harvest and eating the fruit of my words – to become a published author.

I wake up every day filled with peace, joy, and the excitement of starting my own business. God promised to give me witty ideas, creative inventions, and power to make wealth. I have his plan in hand, and baby, I'm working it! I've learned that my real work is what God has given me to do on the earth – to change lives and make eternal impact.

Acknowledgments

I thank God for eternal life and the treasures He's placed in my earthen vessel, for divinely connecting me to Cassandra Washington – whose zest for life is contagious. It caused me to intentionally pursue my predestined purpose. Thank you MJ Schwader for teaching me that vulnerability is key to being a great writer. To King Henry whose love inspired me to unearth the beautiful gift of writing that laid dormant for years.

A Fight From Within: Finding My True Self

By Ilda Grimaldo

"Authenticity is the daily practice of letting go
of who we think we're supposed to be and
embracing who we are." – Brene Brown

On a summer night at the softball field, we decided to celebrate our victory by mingling at the bleachers. As the night progressed, I struck up a conversation with a player I didn't know well. After that evening, we started hanging out and doing things together. She soon became my best friend – and a person who would change my life forever.

As time passed, I realized she hardly spoke about dating. Then one day, she confided in me that she was living an alternative lifestyle. I had never had a friend like "this" before, and I really didn't understand her way of life. What I did understand and the only thing that mattered to me was that she was a good person, with integrity and who held the same family values as I did. With that in mind, her sexual orientation didn't make a difference to me.

We continued our friendship, but after several months it began to develop into a more intriguing relationship. She started to have personal feelings for me, and, surprisingly, I started to have feelings for her, too. I previously had been married for twelve years and divorced for two. Never did I ever imagine that I would have heartfelt feelings for a woman. My life took an interesting turn in what turned out to be the ride of my life.

I soon found myself living a double life. I was dating men and my female friend at the same time. Dating men was natural and socially accepted. And, while dating my female friend was comforting in our own bubbled environment, it was tragic in society. I was living in two worlds, yet felt totally lost in both, and certainly not in control of my life. Worst of all, I was alone with my feelings and my struggle. I couldn't confide in my family or friends because I was afraid of what they might think of me, in addition to what they might say or do.

My journey became extremely challenging as I struggled with my own acceptance of my feelings. It was like riding a wooden roller coaster at 100 miles per hour and it was ready to collapse at any moment. I felt queasy as I screamed for my life.

I longed for the intimacy of my time with my friend. Unfortunately, my self-acceptance was so lacking that although I wasn't an avid drinker I felt I had to be under the influence of alcohol to feel comfortable, content, and fine in the moment. I struggled profusely the mornings after in accepting what had transpired the night before. I felt ashamed, horrible, and nauseated. It became a disturbing cycle and a huge conflict for me.

Because of my struggle with self-acceptance, the fear of being disowned, and having to be dishonest to live my alternative way of life, I made the decision to stop living my double life and decided to do what was socially accepted: a heterosexual lifestyle.

Within a few months I began struggling with my identity again, and found that I was unhappy living the life society expected of me. I desired the love and belonging I felt in the life I had walked away from. One night on my way home, I took a detour to an alternative nightclub. When I walked in, a feeling of relief came over me, with a sense of calmness and a satisfied heart. Although it was a nightclub, it offered a place of comfort. In this place there was no judgment. I could be myself. In that moment, I became crystal clear that this was the lifestyle I yearned for all along. I finally came to terms with my feelings and knew deep in my heart that this was my true self.

Three months later I met a beautiful woman and fell in love. No more mad roller coasters or the need to have alcohol for my intimate feelings. I felt great about my choice to live a life full of love and truth. My family and friends would either accept me for who I was, or not.

My mother was 72 years old at the time. Because we were extremely close and she was my mother, I expected her to accept my new lifestyle right away. I was in love and ready to start my new life, and I wanted her to be a part of my happiness. To my surprise, it didn't turn out the way I wanted it to. I was heartbroken when I realized she was not open to my being gay. It felt like a dagger through my heart, and I was devastated; she was my mom, and she was supposed to be on my side. A year and half passed before she came to terms with my decision to be with a woman. During that time she was concerned about what to say if people asked about me and worried about what people would think. Because of this difficult struggle, she prohibited my partner from visiting their home. Those were extremely difficult times. Although I endured the pain, I still counted my blessings. I was lucky because I was never disowned or unloved by my parents and family, as others have been.

Then one weekend I decided to take a stance against my mother's prohibition. I told her I would stop visiting her and my dad unless I could bring my partner. I was stunned when she didn't change her position. Two months later, I tried again. This time we showed up at their house unannounced. Either they would ask us to leave or welcome us, a risk I was willing to take. When I saw my parents, I hugged and kissed them. Shortly thereafter, my mother welcomed my partner into their lives. It was one of the best days of my life!

Later, I asked my mother what caused her to change her mind. She said it was a sermon she heard one day. She told me it wasn't up to her to place judgment. It was God's place. I would have to deal with Him if He felt it was wrong. Meanwhile, she loved me and only wanted for me to be happy. She could see that I was, and that was enough. I thanked her for her acceptance and blessing as I shed a tear of happiness. Later, after my mother's passing, I received a message that she had regrets about how she had treated us before that day because she realized it is just about love.

Being accepted by my family and friends was awesome. However, it is still a struggle with society. In my "straight" life, I could show public affection to the one I loved. Imagine not being able to demonstrate this type of affection? For 20 years I haven't felt comfortable in public to show how much I love my partner. The stereotypes when they hear the word "gay" immediately relate it to sex. We are real people with real lives and real stories, regardless of our sexual preference. We love our families, friends, co-workers, etc. All we want in return is to be loved unconditionally for our authentic selves and not feel we have to hide our true being.

To fit into society, I compromised my beliefs and sacrificed my happiness. I denied my true self and my deepest feelings. To be my authentic self, I needed to stand in my truth and let the world know that love is love, and we should all embrace that instead of judging others for who they are, or who they love. Even though the alternative lifestyle has come a long way, I'm longing for the day when there is no distinction between gay and straight, and it's strictly about love – unconditional and non-judgmental.

Being authentic when life throws you a curve ball defines your character. Stand in your truth, whatever that truth is, and Be Yourself!

Acknowledgments

I want to thank My Love, Susie, for sharing her life with me and loving and supporting me; my heavenly parents above, and my family, for accepting and loving *me*; my sisters, Joann and Frances, and niece Kali, for their loving support and encouragement to share my story. A special thanks to my friend who helped me realize who I was, to Cassandra for your beautiful guidance and always making me dig deep and be courageous, and MJ for his great coaching skills.

Emerge

Overcoming Obstacles

By Precilla Feliciano Calara

"Any great achievement is preceded by many difficulties and many lessons; great achievements are not possible without them." – Brian Tracy

On an August afternoon seven years ago, my best friend from Canada and her daughter, my niece, my three older children, and my newly baptized, five-week old baby girl, Marian Regine loaded into a van to take a trip from my home in Texas to Matamoros, Mexico. We had decided to go there the day before the Canadians were scheduled to fly home, thinking it would be fun to see a little bit of Mexico.

And then, tragedy struck. Halfway there, my daughter fell asleep at the wheel, and the van rolled several times. When the car finally came to a stop, everyone who had not been hurled from the car was fine. But my baby and I were thrown onto the concrete road. I had a severe cut on my right leg that was bleeding profusely and the left side of my face was swollen and dark. The baby was unconscious. Going in and out of consciousness, I tried to stay awake, convincing myself that it was only a bad dream. But it was real.

I prayed to God, pleading with Him to not take my baby. But that evening, I lost my baby girl.

My husband was working in China when the accident occurred. I still remember having to call him to tell him what had happened and to come home. He flew home immediately and helped me recover. I was at the ICU for three days, then left the hospital to bury my baby.

I had lost my dad, my sister, and my brother, but losing your own child is very, very painful. I felt as though I had died with her. My friends kept telling me to be strong because I still have three beautiful daughters to take care of, and that I needed to be strong for them.

I found myself thinking, *if only I knew that it would happen, we could have just stayed home. If we hadn't gone, I would still have my baby. Why did we have to go there?* In times of tragedy, it is natural to feel regret and denial. But it is only in finding acceptance that we are able to recover. To do that, I finally had to embrace that it might have been my baby's fate to leave so soon, and in doing so, bring our family closer together.

Two weeks after the accident I was scheduled to attend a conference for the network marketing company I work with. I knew that I needed the motivation and the inspiration to rediscover my purpose in life, especially after my loss. I decided to attend, and will be forever grateful that I did. In addition to the warm embrace I received from the leaders and others, I found so much happiness in helping and seeing other people succeed, that being there helped resolve my grief.

My truth is that I made a choice to not focus on the grief and agony. I realized that no matter how long I would grieve, I would not be able to bring my baby back to life. My three daughters needed me, and life was quickly moving forward. In addition, I needed to remain strong while my husband was working away from home. When I accepted what happened and treasured and appreciated my three daughters and my loving husband, I started having peace of mind and much less grief.

But there are times it surfaces. Like when I see little girls who would be the same age as my daughter. To reverse the thought, I thank God for giving her to us for five weeks, appreciating the time we spent with her. I still remember everything, and it still hurts, but I focus on my business and children and that helps.

My daughter Anna, who was driving that day, was deeply affected by the accident. She had only started to drive, and struggled with guilt and depression after the tragedy. I thank God that she is a lot better now, and has found acceptance. Together, we learned to focus our emotions on becoming a strong family, rather than on grief and denial. Because of the accident, she decided to become a doctor so that she can help her family and others live healthier and longer lives. She has been accepted to medical school, and we are so proud of her.

Through all the struggles I have experienced in life – growing up in a poor family in the Philippines, independently building a business, and my family's tragic loss – all happened for a reason. I do not understand why it happened, but with faith in God, I leave it all to Him. He knows what is good for me, and believing in that helps me in every way. I have had loss, but I have also had many blessings.

As the saying goes, God will not give you a challenge that you cannot handle. He is always there to help me. When things do not go how I would like them, I trust that in God's time, it will come to pass.

Because of the accident I became a stronger woman and my family became closer. I found the strength to carry on and achieve my life goals. Through acceptance and appreciation I was able to heal and grow in ways beyond my understanding. For that I'm truly blessed.

Acknowledgments

I would like to thank God for giving me the opportunity to write my story. I would also like to thank my loving husband, Rey, and three beautiful daughters, Anna, Mariel, and Grace. To Cassandra Washington and MJ, thank you for your unwavering love and consistent support that was crucial in completing this book.

Emerge

Strength in My Storm

By Michelle J. Perzan

"In all thy ways acknowledge him,
and he shall direct thy paths."
– Proverbs 3:6

The call from my doctor's office that I had breast cancer changed my life. But not in the way I would have thought. Looking back, I can say it was a blessing in disguise. That's an odd thing to say, but I truly believe that everything does happen for a reason. Some reasons we never fully see come to light; some reasons we see along the way; some we see after we have traveled through them. For me, my learning was in the journey.

Getting a call that you have cancer definitely puts things into perspective. At the time, my boys were 3, 5, and 8. How do you deal with a call like that? It was surreal to think, *What if I die? What if my boys are left without their mama at such a young age? How will my husband handle being a widower at 33?*

In addition, my mom was in hospice, slowly and painfully suffering with bone cancer. She was in my native Canada, so I couldn't see her often. The most difficult thing about my mom having cancer is that she kept everything so secretive, we never knew how to help her. Although she told us four years earlier that she had cancer, I believe she knew before then. When we talked she would never say, *"I have cancer."* She would refer to it as *"the Doctors say this"* or *"my illness."* I asked her why she wouldn't just say that she had cancer. She told me she wasn't going to say that word, that she didn't believe it, and that she would not go the same way her son and husband did.

I can't say I understand what that would feel like, but I do know that when you are facing cancer, you have to own it, say it, and accept it, so that you can fight it, conquer it, and move on. If you can't even say the word, how can you face it and overcome it? I told her there was nothing wrong with saying that she had cancer because it wasn't who she was. It didn't define her or make her any different. She was still amazing, intelligent, and strong. Cancer did not change any of that. I wanted her to face it so we could move on from there.

After seeing her like that, then being diagnosed myself, I knew that I wanted to be open and honest with what was going on with me so that people would know how to help me, or how to pray for me. And just maybe I could help someone see that cancer does not change who you are, it does not define you, and it does not make you a bad person or mean you did anything wrong.

After my diagnosis, I thought of how many people in my family had already passed away from cancer – aunts, my Baba, my brother, my dad, and my mother was dying of it. Was I to be next? Is this where my life ends... suffering like they did, and then losing the battle? I was full of fear.

After the diagnosis, I would drop my boys off at school in the morning and go for a walk and listen to Christian music, especially "I Will Praise You in This Storm". I would cry my eyes out, pray to God for help handling all of this, and ask what I needed to do. I pleaded that I would do whatever He asked if I could be there to watch my boys grow up, graduate, get married, and have children. I wanted to be a grandmother, and I knew I was meant for more than what I had already done. It was at this point, because she was near her own death, that I chose not to tell my mom that her daughter also had cancer. In her situation, that truth would not be necessary.

The walk and cry session became a daily ritual, and as I made my way around the small pond every morning, the clearer things became. I began to notice the beautiful blue sky and the beauty of the tress with the lush green leaves. I could see the blooming flowers and their brilliant colors, and hear the birds and the sounds of life all around me. In the midst of my storm, I began to see the splendor around me, and the blessings that I was missing every day because of my fears.

Each day I was filled with a perfect peace I had never felt before. During those few weeks I learned to be more open about what I was feeling. What I know now is that God had been waiting for *me* to give my burdens and fears to *Him*.

The first test was when I needed to check in to the hospital for my bi-lateral mastectomy. I have no family in town, and we had just started going to a new church three months before. I normally arranged childcare, but this time, my husband Aaron took over. Most of the time, the children were at houses of families that I had not even met. And yet, I felt calm. I had complete trust and faith that God had placed these church families in our lives at the exact time we needed them to help us. By spending those few weeks strengthening myself spiritually, I learned how to let go and be thankful that my three boys were safe and taken care of.

That time was overwhelming for me, in part because my mom was in hospice and because I was afraid of what could happen. Eventually, I broke down and realized that I couldn't do it alone, that I needed others to help me get through all of this. What I learned was my fear was like saying that I don't trust what God can do for me; it was my way of trying to stay safe by a worldly standard, but not by God's.

When I was able to realize that I couldn't do everything alone, my heart turned to a truly thankful one for all that I have. That's when things started to change, in every aspect of my life.

Two days after my double mastectomy, my mom passed away. I had just walked into our home from the hospital still groggy and in pain. As my husband, Aaron, was making me comfortable, the phone rang. It was my sister Julie saying that my mom was gone.

I cried at first, my heart breaking with the loss of my final parent. But in a short time, I smiled. Like all the walks around the pond, God's teaching me to be thankful kicked in. I felt like Mom waited for me to get through the surgery and home safely before she was able to leave this earth. Regardless that I hadn't told her about my cancer, you can call it Mama's intuition; she knew and she wouldn't go until her baby was home safe. That was a precious gift.

I'm still learning daily to know I can trust in the strength and grace that God has given me. I have learned that when you start your day with a thankful heart, that is when God shines His light on you to light your path. Through my faith, I have found peace.

Acknowledgments

I want to first thank God, who has given me strength and courage, but most of all a voice to share how He has blessed me through my trials for being a yielded vessel. I also want to thank my husband Aaron, who always encourages me and pushes me out of my comfort zone; and my wonderful coaches Cassandra and MJ, who pushed me to go deep and be vulnerable.

Silent Tears

By Patricia Alston-Rochon

"Morning light, silk and dreams, take flight
As the darkness gives way to the dawn
You survived, now your moment has arrived
Now your dream has finally been born."
– "Black Butterfly" by Tamia

Every community has its share of characters, secrets, and scandal; small colleges are no different. At first glance, the undergraduate college I attended that was nestled in the rolling hills of the southeast was breathtaking. It sat among acres of well-manicured landscapes filled with plantation-style architecture. The walkways were wide open spaces where people could congregate and watch fellow students stroll to their various destinations. I did not have a care in the world. This was a utopia, or so I thought.

I had stars in my eyes; they were bright and curious. My smile was easy and I walked with confidence. I had admirers, but I did not realize my personal power. Unfortunately, life would soon test my strength in a cruel manner.

I was in college during the era marked by the chaos of Vietnam, the Civil Rights movement, and Women's Rights. There were mock sit-ins on college campuses, and an air of personal response and involvement permeated the air. That's when I first saw him, a self-appointed university activist. I heard his protests about racial discrimination, the war, and white supremacy. This type of behavior was new to me. He seemed like a warrior for the people.

One day as I walked to the library he appeared next to me and introduced himself. I did the same, as we found different seats in separate areas of the common study room. I realized later that he had been watching me.

One evening after a Saturday afternoon football game, I was waiting at the bus depot to return home when I felt his presence from behind. He said my name, then held a knife to my neck and forced me into an open building. There, he and his cousin sexually assaulted me. I was humiliated, afraid of dying, and sickened to the depths of my soul. After they left the area, I ran to the bus depot. I was only eighteen years old.

As I boarded the bus home I could not believe what happened. What was I going to do? I found myself in an inner state of shock. As I rode the bus, I felt betrayed, as if my heart had been cut without visible injury. As I arrived home everything seemed normal. My family did not notice anything unusual about me.

Therein I started my coping strategy by living in denial. I could not face what I thought would be my family's sense of shame. I pretended that nothing had happened. I desperately wanted to be comforted, but I became numb to my feelings. I disassociated myself from the trauma in order to get through each day.

The next day I attended classes. I had a few strange looks, but no one ever questioned me, except for a childhood friend. I responded that nothing had happened to me. She accepted my answer and we remained friends until her death. I tried to speak to the campus Chaplin when I learned that my attackers, who were cousins and drug users, were appealing for money to return home due to the death of their grandmother. While talking to him I mentioned that their appeal was not based in truth. Then, I could not stop crying. College administrators at that time were not especially sensitive to the needs of teary females and innuendos of trouble or conflict. I walked out of his office in total dismay.

My attackers collected enough money to escape, never to return. I felt sometimes that people were talking about me, whispering as I walked by and labeling me as wild, not knowing the true story. If only they really knew. Most people treated me with respect when I guarded my privacy.

I began to lead a double life. I avoided conflict, became secretive, and I took shortcuts to avoid crowds of students and activities. I never flourished in friendships, except for a few people, because I was afraid of rejection and loss of control. I maintained an armor of defense.

I asked my mother if I could transfer to a different school. She was totally against it, so I had to go to classes for three more years. My heart ached and I stayed invisible. But, I was determined to complete my degree. When graduation day finally arrived, I was somewhat fearful when my name was called, then was pleasantly surprised by a rousing applause.

I continued to live in the aftermath of trauma. I found it difficult to verbally commit to a serious relationship with a male. I was in need of counseling, which was taboo for that time. However, I was fortunate enough to work with people who were Christians, and who led by example. They could sense that I was carrying a burden that I needed to work through. I appreciate their patience and nurturing spirit. They were my earthly angels. I also reflected on the biblical lessons learned, the sense of fellowship, and an abiding faith in God that I learned in my childhood Congregational church. I remembered my baby sitter, Ms. Gert. She always called me "her baby". I was surrounded by love. I was grateful for wonderful parents who were devoted to their children. My brothers were sensitive to my nature and I tried to understand them. God in all his glory had provided me with a strong foundation.

During the next decades I married, had two children, obtained a graduate degree, joined professional and social organizations, and became a school administrator and later a hearing officer. I listened to the stories of sexual abuse, sexual harassment, and cruelty. I identified with the cases and vowed to give support, maintain fairness, and provide referrals to counseling agencies. I listened to their stories and I heard in their voices a sense of loss. I acknowledged their feelings and told them to move forward in faith, prayer, and belief in their strength. Gradually, I began to practice what I told others. I kept my inner circle filled with a few people who loved me. I began to forgive myself and live in truth, for I had found my purpose. I opened my heart to others and to my family knowing that God had a plan for my life.

I am alive to rejoice in the amazement of the human spirit. It can survive more than anyone can imagine. I celebrate that I now live in the truth of my life. There are several lifetimes inside me that are waiting to evolve with love. I now live with a spirit of hope, faith, and belief in a higher power; along with an inner strength forged on forgiveness and a new sense of purpose.

Acknowledgments

I want to thank God from whom blessings flow, and my daughter Johanna for encouraging me to tell my story. Also, thank you to all of my earth angels who nurtured and supported me with unconditional love.

The Science of Faith

By Diana Towsley

"Faith is taking the first step even when you don't see the whole staircase." – Martin Luther King, Jr.

I grew up in a family with a scientist father who needed proof for anything's existence, and a mother who prayed to a different saint every day. I wouldn't say I believed in God, as my father questioned me for evidence and as a child I had none. I wouldn't say I didn't believe in God, as my mother dragged my siblings and me to church every Sunday. There was not much inspiration surrounding my experience of God as I grew up. But going to church to see my friends and get donuts was fun, so I continued to go along.

Then my niece was born. Being in the delivery room with my sister as she gave birth to this amazingly perfect little girl moved me like nothing before. I remember thinking that it was a miracle. My sister, my mom, this new life – three generations right in front of me.

When my dad held his first grandchild he wept. I had never seen my dad cry like he did that day. He too was moved. He was holding the proof in his arms of a higher power. There was so much happiness in my family.

At college I found myself feeling lost and lonely. I went to church on campus and experienced a group of really excited people. I wondered if they were doing drugs. None of them could explain why they were so happy. I wanted to feel that way, but I needed something tangible, other than, "I just woke up this way". Why wasn't I feeling the way they were? Why didn't God touch my life like that? Had he forgotten about me?

I graduated college and went on to get a job. I love children and animals, and so I got a job working with children. In the meantime, I kept exploring different avenues of faith. I wanted to believe in a high power, but I had no direct contact. No voice spoke to me, no image showed up in my toast, and yet I still wanted to understand. But nothing. I continued to say my prayers for guidance every night.

Then I met the most amazing man. I told him, "I feel like for the first time in my life God is shining a light on us." We were soon married, and I got pregnant. I lost the baby. Two years later I got pregnant again. I lost the baby again. I decided to change doctors to see if they could explain what was happening. They said I was perfectly healthy. A year passed. I tried to focus on my job, and then I got pregnant again, and I had miscarriage number three.

We were devastated. We had two doctors tell us that they didn't know why, but I probably wouldn't be able to carry a baby full term. I was a healthy, normal woman; I wanted answers, I needed answers. We were told that we should explore other options.

We decided to go down the path of adoption. We met with different agencies, and found one and started the process. My doctor called and said he had a young, unmarried couple that was looking for a family to adopt their soon-to-be-born baby. We were ecstatic, to say the least. We wrote a letter to the couple introducing ourselves, and I created a scrapbook highlighting our life, picking pictures and describing who we were and what we had to offer. The doctor would give what we created to the young couple. I had new hope of being a mom. Even if the baby didn't come from my body, I would be its Mommy.

On the day the doctor was to let us know of the couples' decision, I woke up and decided I was going to go to church. If there were a God, surely he would shine his light on me again and allow this young couple to choose us to raise their baby. My husband did not go with me that morning. I was sitting in church, watching the snowfall outside and praying for the couple to pick us. I remember having a thought cross my mind to not pray for myself, but to pray for the greatest good of everyone involved. That was something I had never thought of before. After waiting all day, the doctor called early in the evening and told us that after much deliberation the couple had decided to get married and keep their baby.

In an instant my dream was shattered again. I was an emotional disaster. I should have been happy. It was, after all, what I had prayed for that morning. I should have been excited for the baby and parents, but instead I screamed and cried.

I didn't want to give up on my dream of being a mom, but I was running out of options. I decided to see a new doctor, a fertility specialist, who didn't know my history. Oh, and he only accepts cash, no insurance. After a few consultations and a few tests we were told he couldn't help us. It was not a matter of getting pregnant; it was a matter of my uterus being able to carry full term.

My husband and I got into a horrible fight that night when he encouragingly suggested we give up our quest and just be happy with all the things we did have. We had exhausted what felt like all of our options. I cried, but this time I screamed to God: "If you exist, which I kind of think you do, please, please take this desire to be a mom away." It was a guttural scream to my core – a pleading. To anyone who has ever had a miscarriage, it is losing a child. All the hopes, wishes, and dreams of holding, guiding, growing, and loving are gone.

I went to bed that night with feelings of hopelessness and despair I had never known. I fell asleep praying, asking for a sign; even an understanding that it wasn't meant to be. Life seemed so unfair, so cruel; this couldn't be the way it was supposed to be. Or was it? I needed help, I needed grace.

When I woke up the next morning nothing extraordinary happened. In fact, you might say it was mundane. I got ready for work just like any other day, except I felt extremely peaceful, with no hopelessness and no despair; just peaceful.

I was asked more painful times than I care to remember, "How many kids do you have?" or "You all don't have kids?" Each time I was asked a question was like a stab to the heart, ripping off my healing wounds. However, one of those questions led to, "Oh, have you heard about the Multiple Miscarriage study?"

I looked into it and found that I needed an answer as to why my healthy body was miscarrying. Because I had three miscarriages I qualified for the study. I showed up to meet with Dr. Branch, a gruff, middle-aged man who briskly told me to stop whimpering. He had a woman in his care that had 29 miscarriages and had just carried a baby full term. I remember thinking, I don't have the strength to go through another miscarriage, and yet, after our first visit with him I had hope again.

I got pregnant again. I miscarried again. And I somehow carried on. But this time we had data: blood tests, hormone levels – scientific, quantifiable data. I was told that my blood was too thick to travel through the umbilical cord. The next time I got pregnant it would be different.

I did get pregnant again and that time I carried full term, delivering a healthy, glorious baby girl. I went to church the morning Gabriella arrived and thanked God for his grace and for his ongoing gift of hope. Even if I didn't understand why things were happening the way they did, I now believed in a higher power. I call that higher power God.

My faith in God has never been stronger. I do believe He heard my screams and my cries. I do believe He was always there with me. I do believe that God has His own timing. I do believe even if I don't understand His will, He has a plan for me.

Emerge

I learned that I needed to be more patient with myself and with others, as we never know all the reasons why something happens.

His image never showed up in my toast. He never spoke to me with words. I do know in my heart when I look with love and compassion at my husband or my daughter, my family, my friends, or even a stranger, God is there. He gifted me the feeling of peace, even if at the time I didn't recognize it as a gift. I've since learned that sometimes our biggest struggles are our greatest gifts, as they mold us into kinder, more patient, compassionate versions of ourselves.

Acknowledgments

Thanks to Jack for countless ways of showing kindness and care, and to Gabriella for the honor of being your mommy. You both make this so much more meaningful – *and* fun!

Thank you to my dad for everything you've taught me, and to my mom for being a great example of a mother, of faith and fun. Thank you to my sister and to my niece Danielle for allowing me to be in your life.

Emerge

38

You Can Live Again

By Suzanne R. Duque

*"Most men lead lives of quiet desperation,
and go to the grave with their song still in them."*
– Henry David Thoreau

Have you ever wondered who you or what your purpose is? Have you ever taken an inventory of your life only to realize that your dreams are now long gone, forgotten, stored away in the depths of your heart?

I would sit in front of my computer, still in my drab gray pajamas, with unbrushed hair, no make up, and looking like I had just crawled from under a rock. Dirty dishes and clutter would pile high on my desk. I was always bone-tired from being up all night defending imaginary castles with imaginary men and chatting with teammates all over the world, making jokes about how their widows must feel since we just sent them to a sudden death.

Then one day, I looked around and realized that I had lost not just weeks or months, but years by playing mindless games on gaming sites just to escape reality. I had become resentful, angry, deeply depressed, and hopelessly apathetic. My corporate job was sucking the life out of me as I worked massive hours, became more stressed, and started to miss important life events. By then, I was taking several depression medications just to get through my day.

I had become my job; it not only defined what I did, it defined me. I felt like I had no reason for living, and because of finances, my lot in life was to work until I died. I even had fleeting thoughts of helping that process along. I was stuck in life with no hope, no dreams, and no answers!

When a friend presented a direct selling opportunity with a network marketing company, I flippantly agreed it was a good opportunity for my husband, Johnny; I knew I had no energy for anything else. For the next 18 months, Johnny watched every video and attended every training to learn about the new business he was building. He tried to engage me, but I didn't want any part of it. Instead, I continued to hide in extensive hours at work and behind the digital walls of virtual reality.

Because Johnny was so passionate, I eventually became curious, and then more involved. I attended a sponsored conference surrounded by positive women and high-energy. Feeling intimidated as I sat at the table with powerful motivational speakers, I was surprised that they saw something more in me. Our conversation planted a seed that I could do something other than what I was doing and have fun doing it. It was the start of a dream that I could live again. I began the search for my purpose, making big investments in books, seminars, and webinars that led to even more questions. The biggest one being, "What's wrong with me?"

The next year, God allowed me to cross paths with the speakers again. When I saw a breakout session with Cassandra Washington on getting in touch with your "why" and your purpose, I thought, *this is what I have been looking for*. I never dreamed that her one session would have such an impact on my life. When I entered the room, there was a feeling of expectation in the air. I was giddy. Cassandra asked us to write down three things that we thought about our lives. I wrote, "Corporate America stole my life, my dreams, and my will to live." There, I had written it! When I looked up, she pointed to me and asked, "What did you write?" So I shared what I wrote. Now, not only had I written it, but I said it out loud. Being honest in front of complete strangers, my emotions overflowed. It was clear this was not the typical session.

I knew this was God showing me a way to change my life. I signed up for Cassandra and MJ Schwader's *Transform Through Writing* program. Doing the writing assignments, old wounds I thought I had dealt with began to surface – the sickening, scared feelings of inadequacy from an abusive first marriage, the death of my parents, the sudden industrial accident that nearly killed Johnny, an embarrassing bankruptcy, and the death of our sixteen year-old son – an event that drove a stake through my heart and ripped my chest wide open and from which I never thought I would ever heal. Life seemed to be one tragedy after another, heaping pain on top of pain. My response to it was to build a wall around my heart so high that *no one* could get over, under, around, or through to hurt me again. I learned to hide it all so well with laughter.

In one of the assignments, I wrote about our son's death and the affect it had on my marriage. After the accident, Johnny emotionally withdrew from me. He was doing the best he could, but he was stuck in time: the day John died. After about five years of this, I said to him that I should have buried him the day we buried John because he was just as dead. Finally, when he did start through the grieving process, I thought things would one day get back to normal, but neither of us were the same after such a tragic loss. Friends, who had also made this journey, let us know that the road was not easy; that most couples end up in divorce. We tried very hard not to let that happen to us, but I would be lying by saying all was good. Johnny and I never seemed to reconnect on the emotional side of our marriage. Oh we laughed, lived life, and had great times, but the gentleness and warmth were gone. I not only grieved over the loss of our child, but I grieved for the relationship we once had. But I had never said a word about it, so he never knew.

The writing allowed me to put my unresolved feelings on paper. Through the writing process, I found the courage to share those feelings with my husband.

I wasn't sure how he would respond or what the results would be. I was always so insecure. I cried as I spoke, and from the pain in his eyes I knew that he had no clue how I felt. Johnny apologized and said he would do better. He told me that he loved me more than anything in the world and never meant to hurt me. I apologized for not sharing my feelings and for letting it go on so long.

After the conversation, I left to go to work and cried all the way. I had a heart-to-heart talk with God. I didn't want to go on this way. God responded and comforted me through the music that played that day. Every song I heard was God telling me everything was going to be okay; that He had this: the finances, the relationships, true happiness, a plan, and a purpose. After lots of tears that seemed to wash my soul I surrendered and let God have it all. When I got home Johnny and I vowed that we would begin again.

For years, I hid my voice and myself from the world and from life. Without this writing program, I would have never had the courage to open up to Johnny. We would have just continued on the same path. I don't know if I would have ever said anything at all. Because of the abuse from years ago, I've always been hesitant to disagree with him and instead kept my mouth shut. Since then, Johnny has responded to my needs and I've tried to do things that I know makes him happy, too.

Our conversation was like a dam breaking, and even more old ugly thoughts and feelings came gushing out. The more I wrote, the clearer things became, but also more questions, deeper questions came. It's a scary feeling when you face things that you thought you buried forever. I realized that some of my hurt came from not trusting God. There have been some wonderful times in my life, but I couldn't see them because I was so deep inside my walls of pain and fear. I had always felt I wasn't "good enough" or "worthy" of God's blessings, but today is a new beginning.

Now after years of trying to figure out who I am, I feel that I am finally discovering my purpose: To be God's messenger of love, forgiveness, and trust; to help others through the muck and mud of their lives. Have I completely got it all figured out? Absolutely not, and that's okay. God and I have a song that is mine and mine alone, and if I don't sing it, then no one else will.

My prayer is that you will seek to find your purpose, your true calling that will bring true happiness. Once you find that, I know you will discover that life is worth living and God's exceedingly abundant blessings above all that you could ever desire or pray for will find their way into your heart.

Acknowledgments

I would like to give praise to God and thank Him for loving me. He is my rock, my shield, my savior and my song. I would also like to thank my wonderful, amazing husband, Johnny; without his loving support and encouragement this chapter would have never been written. You are my soulmate, my lover, and my friend. Thanks, honey, for allowing me room to grow. Last, I want to thank Cassandra Washington, my sister in Christ. God put you in my path for a reason and I have been blessed beyond measure because of it.

Emerge

Finding My Way

By Susan W. Corbran

"Rejoice in hope, be patient in tribulation,
be constant in prayer." – Romans 12:12

The closing prayer began as I tentatively reached for the hand of the man who stood next to me. I had admired him for some time, having watched him take care of his dying wife. At that moment something deep inside me came alive, a stirring, a knowingness, and the thought popped into my head: He could be my knight in shining armor and I could be his princess! But when I stepped up to the plate, it wasn't as a princess, but as a damsel in distress. As a single parent raising three kids, I was struggling. Although I had wanted to prove to myself I could do it on my own, I needed help.

Barry needed help as well, as he was raising his own three girls. What started as an innocent way to share advice, turned into a race to see who would send the first email. As the months passed, we realized our friendship had become a relationship. Although our kids had hoped for a longer engagement, we were married four months after he proposed. I was finally feeling like the princess with all my dreams coming true.

My prince would leave love notes on my pillow or a singing message on my phone when he left early for work. Not a day would go by without saying, "Have I told you lately how much I love you?" It was my love for him that sent me to get my hunting license. I discovered his secret about spending so much time in the stand; it was to be with God. The stand was a safe haven, a place with no worries, no stress, no problems; only time to pray or meditate. There were times when I would go there, even if it wasn't deer season, just to pray and seek His guidance, such as when our house burned down. I continued to thank God for giving me Barry, for he was the one I wanted to be married to for the rest of my life.

Then one day my world was turned upside down. I wanted to run to the deer stand and hide, but we weren't home, we were at the doctor's office. I was holding tightly to Barry's hand as we were given the news that he had an incurable cancer. My head was swirling with thoughts: Why was this happening to us? God knew that we loved Him and would do anything for Him. Hadn't we dedicated our new house to Him? What was I going to do? How would I support myself? I was dependent on Barry for everything.

That first night I prayed that God would take me instead, so that Barry's girls wouldn't become orphans. We knew God was in control; we just didn't want to believe that this was part of His plan.

God was with us during the eighteen-month journey. Somewhere along the way, our roles started to change, though Barry wasn't ready to give up being the main provider. I continued to drive him to his sales appointments. As a caretaker, I watched his body drop in weight and weaken. I was frightened one night when he fell out of bed. I thought he had died, but then he was jarred awake and climbed back into bed. The not knowing of when he would die, or how it would take place was nerve-wracking. I just didn't want to miss the opportunity to hold him and pray him into heaven.

While Barry was at the hospital receiving fluids, I had a chance to talk to his doctor and ask him how much time Barry had left. After hesitating, he told me maybe two weeks. I went to Barry's side and held his hand and said, "The doctor said you could go home tomorrow as long as we sign up with hospice."

"Hospice?" he replied. "I didn't know I was that bad."

The tears rolled down my face as I cried. "The doctor says you only have two weeks left to live." I leaned over him and hugged him. I didn't want to let him go. While at home, he spent time with each of his girls and with me. We kept him comfortable and by the end of that first week, he had drifted off in his sleep to heaven while we sang his favorite song, *Victory in Jesus.*

I became numb. Then my heart ached so much it felt like it was split in half. I just wanted to curl up and die. The tears flowed almost constantly. I never imagined how hard this journey would be; and although I knew others would travel this road, I didn't wish it upon anyone. I filled my calendar with lots of activities and spent time traveling to visit the grandkids. I was stuck in a rut, spending my savings with no goals laid out for myself.

I knew I needed to start taking care of myself and get a job, but I had lost my confidence when Barry died. So I went back to the deer stand and spent time with God.

With several counseling sessions behind me, I was beginning to understand the grief process. I spent some time writing a letter to Barry, thanking him for our time together, apologizing for things I had done, forgiving him for things he had done, and sharing things that were left unsaid. And then I wrote good-bye. It was very therapeutic, and although it helped me start the healing process, I still wasn't at the place where I was ready to support myself. As the year continued, I made investments, such as joining groups that focused on personal development.

During a private coaching call I was asked: What are your goals? What is your truth? What does it look like to stand in your truth? And so forth. I was embarrassed. I had no idea what I was supposed to be doing. I felt like I had been swallowed up in a thick fog with no clear direction in sight. I had spent so much time doing for others over the years that I forgot what it was like to do things for myself. I had just never imagined I would ever be among unfamiliar surroundings.

But I knew I wasn't alone, for God was with me, every step of the way. At just the right moment, He opened the door to my passion for writing. Although I had kept a journal off and on over the years, I never took the opportunity to have something published. Writing with this group has become a dream come true. I believe God wants us to share our pain, trials, and struggles to help and encourage others along the way.

Even though approaching Barry's anniversary in heaven brings back tearful memories, it's also an opportunity to see how far I've come since his death. I know there will be grief throughout my life, but I have decided not to let it define me. After Barry died, I was stumbling, trying to find my way; two years later I am gaining back my confidence, knowing this verse: "I can do all things through Christ who gives me strength" (Philippians 4:13).

As I trust God for the things that will support me through this life, I'm taking this opportunity to share even more stories. I now have my own website – www.suecorbran.com, which highlights not only my work, but life experiences as well. I have several files of stories (childhood on up to adulthood) sitting on the sidelines, waiting to be refined and printed into a book titled *Around Robin Hood's Barn*. And with my love of traveling, I'm hoping to take trips off the beaten path to meet my neighbors and listen to their stories, so I can add them to my books and share with many more people.

Already God has allowed for the words to flow out and provide much healing, as well as comfort and peace. Others who have walked in my shoes of grief are thanking me for sharing my experiences. My prayer is that those who read my stories will be strengthened. And so my story continues.

Emerge

Acknowledgments

I want to thank God for the gift and passion to write; my coaches Cassandra and MJ for helping me break down the walls to become the writer God created me to be; and my late husband Barry, for he always taught me to follow my dreams.

Emerge

A Surprise Visitation

By Maria "MJ" Martinez

*"Forgiveness is unlocking the door to set someone free
and realizing that you were the prisoner."*
- Unknown

I don't have many childhood memories of my father. He left
our family in Mexico to find work in the U.S. when I was only
seven. I was his first child and he and I always held a special
bond. After he left us, my father sent money and letters, often
making promises he never fulfilled. After several years, my
father moved from California to Texas and his communication
was less, until finally, it was no more. His broken promises
caused hardships for my mother, and my feelings toward him
grew hostile. He had forsaken me, and I could not find it in my
heart to forgive him.

Because my mother was a single parent raising my four
siblings and me, at times we struggled financially, so I started to
work at age 16 to help her. Mother was a devout woman, and
raised us to be people of integrity, teaching us about religion
and tradition. We learned to pray to the Virgin Mary and to
saints, but I thought God was even more distant than my father.
"How could a God so far away care about me?" I wondered.

With each passing birthday, I harbored more negative
feelings toward my father. I was full of anger and resentment.
Hatred was a cancer in my heart. In search of my identity, I
began to ask questions my mother couldn't answer. My most
burning question was, "Why would the person I loved the most
vanish from my life?" He missed the things fathers do with their
children, like taking us to the park, attending school events, or

simply getting an ice cream and talking. I always dreamed of having a relationship with my father where we could talk about anything. I felt incomplete without him.

One day a pretty little book with a flower on its cover arrived in the mail; it was a New Testament Bible. Neither my mom nor I knew who sent it, but it was easy to read, and I was intrigued by the letters from Paul the Apostle, especially the verse in Philippians 4:13 – "I can do all things through Christ who strengthens me." I was puzzled. "How can Jesus help me if he is hanging on a cross?" So inspired by this little book, I put God to the challenge. If God is real, I prayed, prove it by taking me to visit my father in Texas.

Travel to the U.S. at that time was not easy. First, I needed finances and a passport, and then I was required to travel to Guadalajara to get a visa at the American Consulate. Logic told me that it would never happen. I did not have the money or the necessary paperwork they asked for. However, the verse I read in Philippians came to my mind many times through the process, giving me hope.

Then a miracle! What had taken others many months, took me less than the time I stood in line. Amazingly, everything I needed fell into place. Looking back on it now, the ease at which my tourist visa was approved was the beginning of my faith in God. I resigned from my job to prepare to go, and quite unexpectedly, I received a severance check for my seven years of service, giving me the finances to afford the journey.

As I traveled to California to visit relatives, then to my brother's house in Arizona, and from there to my father's house in Texas for a month-long visit, I was filled with so many mixed emotions. I was angry and bitter, yet excited to see my father again.

When I finally met my father at the airport, he hugged me tight for a long time. To my amazement, that one embrace healed years of pain. My plan was to confront him about his absence and lack of support, but oddly I couldn't. It was as if my lips were sealed between the fingers of God.

When I arrived at my father's home, I could see that he lived alone. His house was modest and close to his job, where he worked the evening shift. During the day my father lavished me with gifts, taking me shopping for clothes and music. I felt special again and his affection almost made up for all the years we missed together. He introduced me to his friends and reacquainted me with family, and on some days he and I simply spent peaceful time together. The weeks flew by so quickly, I didn't want our visit to end. My heart was filled with gladness.

Then one night, as I sat alone watching television while my father was at work, there was an insistent knock at the door. When I answered the door, two women were standing in front of me. The older lady asked, "Who are you and what are you doing here?" When I explained that I was visiting my father, she screamed, "You can't be his daughter because he doesn't have any children!" I replied, "I don't know what my father has told you, but he has a wife and five children who love him very much." As the conversation continued and the truth that my father had hidden from me was revealed, the scab of my old wound was ripped off.

The lady said she would return later to get to the bottom of it. Crying, angry, and in shock, I had been betrayed by him again. I wanted to leave as fast as I could, but because I wanted to spare my mother and siblings from the anguish I felt inside, I had no one to call and no one to console me.

When my father arrived from work early the next morning, my fervent anger met him at the door. The woman returned too. I couldn't believe the soap opera that was playing out before me. I was heartbroken; the anger that disappeared during our embrace just three weeks before returned, crashing my soul like a tidal wave hitting the shore and destroying all of the beauty of its surroundings.

"I want to leave now!" I declared. My father begged me to stay. To my displeasure, I had to give in because my return ticket was scheduled one week later. During those final days, my dad and I were more distant than ever. Eating together or do any activity was like adding salt to an open wound. "God if you are real why is this happening!?" I cried.

The emotional pain in my heart was at its highest point. All of the feelings of abandonment I felt as a child weighed on me like a large sack of rocks. After my return to Arizona, I sought refuge at my brother's church. During the service, we prayed the Lord's Prayer, a prayer I'd recited since childhood. But at the point of the prayer that says "forgive us our trespasses as we forgive those who trespass against us," I felt a strange tug at my heart. "How could I forgive him after all he has done?"

I can't explain why, but after the prayer my heart felt softer, although it still ached. I was miserable and I wanted to feel better, so I registered to attend a spiritual retreat the following weekend.

The retreat began with praise and worship and singing that I hadn't experienced in Mexico with my mom during Mass. As the songs played, my heart was filled with joy, even as the heartbreak lingered. There were no images of saints or the Virgin Mary, but the singing created an atmosphere of reverence. It was a devotion that helped me understand God's love for me, and I opened my heart to receive God's forgiveness. I could not hold on to the anger and pain anymore.

As others prayed for me, they prayed "in Jesus's name," without using Virgin Mary or any other saints. I hadn't heard this phrase in prayer before. I stood with my eyes closed and went on a journey from my mother's womb to each hard moment that marked my life until that day, and suddenly, all the bitterness and hurt left me; my heart was lifted like a butterfly in flight. I cried like a river, my tears like medicine for my soul.

After the prayer, I saw a vision of Jesus on the cross, an image I'd seen every day in my mother's living room, only this time Jesus stepped down from the cross and walked toward me with his hands extended. His clothes turned from a dingy loincloth to a beautiful, shimmering white robe. As Jesus walked toward me, I shouted in a loud voice, "God is real! God is real!"

Until that moment, my hatred for my father had kept God at a distance. I was blinded by my un-forgiveness, and my religion and tradition too. But, the vision was clear and the healing that was taking place in my heart proved that God was real. In that moment, I knew the visit with my father had led me to this divine moment.

After that day my life changed. The seed of forgiveness was beginning to bloom and for the first time, I truly released the resentment I'd held for so long.

A few years later I met my dad again, which culminated my inner healing forever. I asked him to forgive me, and I told him that I forgave him. I explained that God had changed my heart and given me a new life. My father wept openly. As I sat beside him, I held his hand, for I knew the tears were medicine for his soul.

Over the years, I have learned to accept my father as he is. We talk on the phone occasionally, and I tell him that I love him – words that are more real in my heart than ever before.

Since this incident, God continues to be my greatest inspiration. I'm no longer carrying the burden I held since childhood. My cup is filled with joy, and I can say that the power of forgiveness gives me the strength to love. My prayer for you is that God allows your heart to forgive and your cup runs over with love.

Emerge

Acknowledgments

First of all I want a give thanks to God. I also want to thank Cassandra Washington and MJ Schwader for helping me to tell my story exactly with the right words, and for publishing this book. God bless you both!

Healing Through Forgiveness

By Sandra Brooks

"Emerson said, 'Do you love me?' means 'Do you see the same truth?' – or at least, 'Do you care about the same truth?'" – C.S. Lewis

One spring morning, I got a call from a dear friend. After talking for a while, she heard the smoke detector beeping in the background and said, "It's time to change your batteries." I replied casually, "Yes, I guess it is." After we got off the phone, I faded back into the numbness of everyday life, tuning out the beeping noise altogether.

About six months later, the same friend called again. Right away, she noticed the beeping sound in the background. "Girl, you still haven't changed the batteries in that smoke detector?" I could hear her concern. Then it hit me like a ton of bricks. I was shocked and ashamed at the lack of attention I had paid to something so easy to fix. I honestly had not heard the beeping until she mentioned it again. For six whole months, I had moved throughout my house without even noticing that annoying sound.

I knew then that something was terribly wrong. After hanging up the phone, I couldn't change the smoke detector batteries fast enough. It was shortly after this profound realization of how "unconscious" I had become that a series of life-changing events began to unfold.

Though it may sound like a fairy tale, this is my story. After 20 years of marriage, I was not happy. My husband repeatedly lied about his infidelity, and although I loved him and stayed with him for the sake of the children, it became harder and harder to trust him.

And then, on a cold January night, I once again found myself faced with a choice: stay with him or leave for good. I chose to stay. It seemed like the easiest thing to do. I wanted to start over in our marriage, despite the quarrels. So, I tried to forget all the previous arguments, denying the truth. I kept telling myself, *I love him, and I want to make this work.*

Family is important to me. I did not have a stable family life growing up and I wanted so much for my children to have the stability I had always longed for. So I vowed to make my marriage work, even though my husband was unfaithful again and again. Deep inside myself, I knew I was fighting a losing battle but, for my family's sake, or so I told myself, I chose to close my eyes to the truth that was screaming to be heard. Then it all came crashing down one evening.

I cuddled up against him as I always did, and I felt hope again. As I caressed his back, I leaned over to look into his eyes and said, "I love you." He replied that he loved me too. A few seconds later the phone rang, breaking the spell of my sweet moment. He answered the phone and his face immediately changed as he subtly pulled away. As he fumbled his words, I knew he didn't want me to hear his conversation. He slowly moved the phone to the other ear, as if I wouldn't notice. He tried to end the call, but I was already alarmed. I snatched the phone from his hand and demanded to know who was on the other end of the line.

"Who do you want to speak to?" It was obvious that the caller was trying to disguise his voice, and, stuttering, he blurted out a name I didn't recognize. I was furious now and angrily demanded, "Did you call to speak to my husband?" The voice on the other end of the phone replied, "I'm sorry I think I have the wrong number," and hung up. As angry as I was, I was even more hurt. My heart was broken again, as always. I felt so foolish to believe him once more.

Trembling with rage, I redialed the number, and this time a woman answered the phone. Her voice sounded sassy. I said, "You just called my husband's cell and I want to know why you're calling him?" My heart was pounding so hard I was sure she could hear it. I wasn't used to trusting my intuition, and since my husband refused to be honest, I wanted someone to tell me the truth.

"I'm married," the voice on the other end replied. "I have a man and I don't need yours!" I thought her loud, defensive tone and smart-aleck response was a lie. Confused, I sharply hung up the phone and I knew my fantasy of a happy marriage was crushed.

I could no longer pretend. Over the next few months, I withdrew from family and friends, and I went into a deep depression. I ranted that life was not fair. I was unable to imagine any life outside the "happy family of four" fantasy that I had fooled myself into believing for so long. *How can it be like this? This is not my perfect ending. Where is my happily ever after?*

Then my thoughts turned viciously inward. Maybe I needed to lose weight, change my hair, or maybe I was too available to him, or not available enough. I blamed myself and asked, "What could I have done to make him love me and want me more?" Although I tried to deny it, I finally came to the realization that there was nothing I could have done to change *him*.

So I kept my distance as I tried to figure out what I was going to do for me. How was I going to deal with this? In the past, my excuse for staying had been my kids, but my children were grown up and soon out of the nest.

All my life, all I have ever been was a wife and mother, which I had allowed to totally define me. Roles were attached to me like strings to a puppet, and one-by-one they were being cut off. I felt like I had traveled to a foreign country and I didn't speak the language.

I had two options: I could accept the situation as it was and continue to live with blinders on for another 20 years, or I could embrace this new sense of awareness. I chose the latter. I am choosing to be kind to myself, accepting what I can change, and letting go of what I can't. And, I am getting better at recognizing the difference.

For now, I am still married, gaining the self-confidence and the financial means to stand on my own. I am getting to know myself though counseling and my *Transform Through Writing* community.

I am no longer denying the reality of my husband's cheating. And, my husband is now being honest with me about his past infidelity, which I appreciate. What matters is that I get it loud and clear.

I'm learning to appreciate the time I have with family and friends, and most importantly the time I spend with myself, which has always been a very big hurdle for me. One very important thing that I'm learning is that I can't change anyone else; I can only change myself. So, I am learning about me. What I value; my likes and dislikes. My first step led me to awareness, triggered by a long ignored alarm. I now choose to live consciously.

And, I'm forgiving my husband and forgiving myself because it's important for my well-being – spiritually, physically, and emotionally. Forgiveness does not mean that I condone or accept my husband's behavior. I do not. It means allowing him to be who he is and not putting expectations on him that are beyond his capabilities. He has to decide whether he will change or not. For many years, I held onto hurt and rejection. Forgiveness is bringing peace and clarity to my life. And I realize that I am capable of changing the end of my story.

Acknowledgments

I would like to acknowledge my writing community. Thank you for supporting me by phone and text. Thank you to my family for supporting me, as well. Also, thank you Cassandra for all your help, love, and support.

Let Go and Let God!

By Gillian Smith

"We attain freedom as we let go of whatever does not
reflect our magnificence. A bird cannot fly high or far
with a stone tied to its back. But release the impediment,
and we are free to soar to unprecedented heights."
– Alan Cohen

Joe and I met in an upscale mall years ago. I was a specialist
working in the department store selling men's designer suits. At
the time, Joe was one of my customers and would always wait
for me until I was available to assist him with what he wanted to
purchase. He was obviously interested in something more than
clothing.

A year and a half later, after moving to the other side of
town, I bumped into Joe and a friend of his. We exchanged
phone numbers, and he called and asked me out on a date.
Although I had mixed feelings, I was not ready to come out of
my comfort zone to date him or anyone else. I informed Joe
that I was interested in being friends, but that anything more
would not work for me.

My reluctance came from having been through so much in
my short life. I was a young widow with two children and I was
living my life. Joe and I kept in touch, but eventually I moved to
the east coast and we lost touch.

One day about six years later, the phone rang. To my
surprise it was Joe. When I asked him where he was, he said,
"I'm right around the corner!"

This time the connection developed into a great relationship, and things were, as you would say, "Marvelous in paradise."

Because Joe's work involved television and travel, we got to see each other quite a few times that year. We were courting, and that was not what I had planned. I had dedicated my life to the Lord years ago, and knowing that Joe was a little wild, I did not want to get mixed up with anything remotely close to this type of relationship. However, Joe seemed changed. There was something about him that was different. He actually began going to church when he got back from traveling.

We traveled from coast to coast that year, experiencing all types of scenic beauty, from coastlines to mountains to sunsets. That Christmas, Joe sent tickets for my children and me to come out to California. We flew out and had a wonderful holiday. On Christmas Eve, as we finished our meal, Joe handed me a fortune cookie for dessert. When I opened my cookie a beautiful princess-cut gold ring appeared. Joe asked me to marry him that night, and I accepted. I was ecstatic, laughing, and bubbling over with joy.

A few months later, Joe and I decided to relocate the entire family to California. Joe and I traveled to Hawaii for our wedding on a private beach at the Ritz Carlton, where we enjoyed chocolate covered strawberries and champagne. We traveled around the islands, seeing beautiful rainbows and other wonderful sights.

Then reality set in. Joe had a lot of fear that he hadn't dealt with before the wedding. I had a lot of insecurities and hurt from my past as well. Having not dealt with our personal issues before we married, not even giving these issues the serious attention that they needed after we were married, our ship was unknowingly headed to a major crash. It happened quickly.

By the time I gave birth to my third and last child, my marriage was stormy. We drifted apart and it seemed the longer we were married, the more he traveled and worked, and the busier I was being Supermom.

I began to ask myself why I believed anything he said to me, even from the beginning. We did everything possible, including going to counseling, which only delayed the inevitable.

I filed divorce papers, but Joe begged me to wait. I agreed, and unbeknownst to me, Joe deviously took the equity out of the home we shared, among other underhanded tactics he did. It got incredibly ugly from there on.

I learned many lessons from my choices. First, a good friend should stay in the good friend category. Being friends then lovers is hard when it doesn't work, because you end up losing both.

Another learning is that it is important to follow your first mindset. My first inkling was not to date this man. But I got sucked in, and everyone in the equation experienced pain.

I also learned to break the barriers and chains that kept me silent. He found joy in the verbal beat down; I found peace in the word of God. I also found that I needed to stand in my truth and follow my heart.

The most important lesson of all was to love myself. I saw in him a person who didn't love himself, so how could he love anyone else? And in that reflection, I saw that I needed to pay attention to who I was. And that meant to look deeply at who I am and what my purpose is on earth.

Although it took years to accept him for who he is and to let go of the animosity I had for him, I have learned forgiveness and trust. I fought a great fight to keep my children and myself positive and flowing in a new life, and I succeeded. My children are all thriving and doing well. I have my own business and ministry, speaking to many men and women on a national level. Since letting go of him, I have not looked back.

I'm constantly re-evaluating myself now, engaging in self-development activities to expand myself and staying on purpose by using my gifts to benefit the world. I am fixed on completing my destiny and now I'm free to achieve it! I can, because I decided to love myself, first.

Acknowledgments

First of all I would like to give God all of the Glory, without Him I would not have made it through! I am sending many thanks to beautiful and supportive Mary Jean, Jeff for his encouragement, and Ms. Stephanie for her patience with me. A very special thanks to Coaches MJ and Cassandra; your guidance and coaching is God sent. May the Lord richly bless you on this journey.

Climbing Into the Sweet, Clean Air

By Elizabeth Corbell

"The gates of Hell are open night and day
Smooth the descent, and easy is the way
But to return, and view the cheerful skies,
In this the task and mighty labor lies."
– Virgil

I woke up one morning and found myself living in Hell. It began when I converted to Catholicism. My parents could not accept that I had found a close connection to God outside the faith I was raised in. They showed up on Easter Sunday saying they couldn't stop me from joining the church of the devil, but they were going to rescue their grandchildren and make sure they were brought up in the right church. I said no, and there began the descent.

Then I developed medical problems that caused intense, constant pain; I was soon taking up to eight Vicodin a day without relief. I thought I should be nominated for sainthood because I got out of bed in the morning and cared for the children all day, but my husband also wanted a spotless house and dinner on the table every night. He started saying things like he could love me, but didn't because I hadn't done enough for him. It seemed like no matter how hard I tried after that, I was never quite good enough to earn his love. Then he started denying me my medicines. And if I complained, I was told how selfish I was to expect money to be spent on me, instead of the entire family.

So there I was. I had no love from my husband, and lots of disapproval from my parents; excruciating pain, but no medicines to stop it. And there was no help taking care of the children, no matter how sick I was. That's when I found myself definitely living in Hell. I didn't think I deserved it and I was very angry, especially at God. How could I believe in a loving, caring God when He let me suffer like this? That was the absolute closest that I ever came to committing suicide, because I saw no way out. Living in Hell is the absolute, abject hopelessness of ever escaping. The only reason I didn't kill myself at that time was because I loved my children and I thought they needed me, even if I believed no one else did.

But God did hear me, and he brought Father Aidan into my life. Like Christ, Father Aidan taught me that I was valued, and my value did not stem from what I could or could not do. It stemmed from the fact that I was God's daughter. I could have a good life – not just after I died – but here and now. Father Aidan brought hope back into my life.

Then he helped me to graduate from spiritual childhood. Gradually, over time, my prayers changed. Instead of asking God to change Sonny, I started praying *for* Sonny. Instead of whining about my life, I asked God to help me see what I could do to make things better.

I started with my parents. Daddy would pop off and say any hurtful, insulting, or embarrassing thing he felt like and it didn't matter who was around. After an incident at our son's first birthday party, where Daddy kept saying inappropriate things, I finally asked him to leave. For the first time ever, Daddy had to face the consequences of his own bad behavior. I wouldn't put up with it any longer.

Sonny was a different matter entirely. I loved him, despite his cruel treatment of me. Another thing Father Aidan helped me to see was that the anger I felt toward God was a measure of my belief in God. If I didn't believe in God, I couldn't very well be angry at Him, could I? But that argument applied to Sonny as well. I could tell *exactly* how much I loved Sonny by how deeply he had hurt me. So I got a job outside the home and had my own money. Sonny tried various tactics to get it and would demand my entire paycheck, but I stood my ground and said no, it wasn't his to spend. I got my prescriptions.

So everything was moving ahead. All I had to do was stand up for myself a few times and suddenly I had everyone's love and respect and we all lived happily ever after, right? Hardly. It took years. My parents and Sonny waited for me to make a mistake, to back down, to waver just a little bit. Sometimes I gave in because I'd been in pain for days and just didn't have the energy to fight. Sometimes I'd make a loving gesture and it would be taken as a sign of weakness. So it wasn't easy, it wasn't steady, and it definitely wasn't quick. But it was progress.

Unfortunately, I could not hide from myself. I was miserable and deeply wanted to be loved, but wasn't. You know that term "heartache"? I thought it was a euphemism for feeling really sad. But if you cry hard enough for long enough, you will feel an ache right over your heart. And I felt it every day for over a year. I didn't want to cry anymore, but I didn't know how to stop.

Then one morning it suddenly dawned on me that I wasn't the first woman in history to be married to a man who didn't love her. I looked at my life. I had three wonderful children who loved me. I had a great job. I had a church I liked, where I volunteered. Shock swept through me as I realized that *I had a good life!* And then another thought: *Everyone* has something about their life they wish they could change. This was my something. I quit mourning over what I *didn't* have and started being grateful for what I *did* have. It was a slow process, but I began to heal. The day came when I stopped crying.

Gradually life got better. My parents learned to respect me as an adult. Things got better with Sonny, too, and for six years we lived amicably together, but as roommates. My health gradually improved and the day arrived when I didn't need Vicodin any longer.

One day, Sonny came to pick me up from work and I was unusually quiet. He asked me what was wrong. I said I'd realized I had no one to miss me when I died. He said the children would miss me. I said they would miss their mother, but that wasn't the same thing as missing *me*, the woman who collected frogs, who thought math was relaxing, who thought Godzilla movies were the greatest – there was no one to miss *her*. And then Sonny said *he* would miss me, and that surprised me because I really didn't think he would. Later, I asked him if he wanted to try again at our marriage, but he blew up and said he still had anger issues and he was going to have to see some changes first.

That evening I wrote him a long, loving letter. Basically, I said I wasn't interested in earning his love; he either loved me or he didn't. I'd given him what he wanted most in life – two daughters and a son, and they were almost grown. I would move out and he would finally be rid of me. I lay the letter on his pillow and went to my room and cried most of the night.

The following day he said he didn't want me to go. I asked, "But do you love me?"

He said, "Well, it's really hard for me to admit it, but I suppose I do."

"All right. I'll stay."

And that was all we said. Sonny announced it to the children that we were starting over, and he's been as good as gold ever since. I think he must have been on his own journey, because the old Sonny would have helped me pack. But the new Sonny is courteous and kind and tells me that he loves me. If he hurts my feelings, he apologizes. After 25 years of marriage, we finally found true love.

So God did hear me and bless me. But it wasn't until I learned to stop praying *about* the people in my life and to start praying *for* them, when I learned to stop complaining about what I didn't have and to start giving thanks for what I did have. That is both when and how God led me out of Hell. For Virgil it was seeing the sky again. For me, it's like walking outside of a smoke-filled prison room after many years and taking that first, deep breath of crisp, clean air. It's so refreshing, so sweet. Like Heaven.

Acknowledgments

I would like to personally thank Darcie Beyer for making it possible for me to be part of this project. Not only did she invite me to participate, but she also sponsored me so I could accept. I also wish to thank Allison McFadden for her invaluable assistance in editing my chapter. She was a life-saver!

Emerge

Standing in My Truth

By Johnnene Gay

"Life for me ain't been no crystal stair."
– Langston Hughes

Late one night at a conference, I saw a man sneaking a candy bar and a yogurt while his wife was in bed. It was after 10 pm, and this grown man in his 60's felt the need to sneak treats to comfort a desire. As I watched him, it dawned on me that it's not just me who did these things. And it's not just women who fight food wars. I needed to see this man do the same thing I did to know it's real for others, not just me; that people experience mind games over food.

For years I've dealt with a mental comparison, thinking that there was something wrong with me that I couldn't focus enough to do what I needed to do. It didn't help me to know that diabetes, heart disease, and high blood pressure runs in my family. It didn't matter to me that I was borderline glucose sensitive, and that if I didn't make a lifestyle change, I could end up with diabetes. None of that knowledge sunk in enough for me to change how I felt about my body.

Negative self-talk goes hand-in-hand with a negative self-image. I don't remember when I started comparing myself to other women, holding myself to a standard of beauty, size, and weight that was unattainable. I often felt like I was a failure because I was not able to meet that standard, even with all the effort I put into it. I was always in a mode of perfectionism, always on guard, watching everything I ate, tracking my every move.

I didn't allow myself to eat what I wanted, instead spending time analyzing what to eat, measuring and weighing my food to assess good and bad options for consumption. I spent so much energy on this that I didn't put as much thought into other things, like my normal day-to-day demands of keeping organized and tidying my house. I had no desire to tackle the mounds and baskets of paper that I needed to sort through. I couldn't think about one more thing other than my obsession with food and the size of my body.

I'm not sure when and why I became self-conscious. In high school and college, I got a lot of unwanted attention from older guys and men because of my curves. I wanted a body shape like the other girls; I wanted to be popular. I wanted to be smart and noticed by the boys my age for more than my body. I don't remember a time I didn't get attention from older guys, but I can remember in high school wanting more attention from guys my age. Did I subconsciously put on extra weight to try and discourage this unwanted attention?

Besides feeling like a failure, I felt "less than" other women. I didn't feel like I sized up to their beauty, which caused me to push harder to change my physical appearance. I told myself that I had to do more, but deep down I knew I'd never measure up. It showed up in my eating, constantly dieting, and counting calories. It also showed up in my relationships, with my thinking that there is something more that I could be doing to make my husband happy. That thinking was as exhausting as trying to eat right and exercise.

As a result, I had a hard time believing God's promises for me, that I am made perfect in His image; that I am beautifully and wonderfully made. I would read scripture daily, but I never made the connection that God was talking about me; that I could rest in His plans for me. My favorite scripture, Jeremiah 29:11 (NIV), never permeated my heart: "For I know the plans I have for you, declares the Lord. Plans to prosper you and not to harm you, plans to give you hope and a future." What it proved to me was that reading the material is not the same as meditating on and understanding what is written.

What made me want to live in someone else's body, walk in someone else's shoes? It's taken me my entire life to this point to acknowledge that I'm a work in progress, but that I too have something to contribute to society. God didn't design me to be shaped exactly like Jane, to have flowing hair like Barbara, to have a picture perfect smile like Denise. He created me in His image to be Johnnene.

Writing this chapter helped me realize that I didn't appreciate myself. I also realized that everyone has something going on in his or her life. That knowledge has helped me become more relaxed and less self-condemning. There is a part of everyone's life that they are not satisfied with.

Despite my long history of searching, my transformation didn't truly occur until I started counseling. My therapist asked questions that resulted in the truth staring me in the face. Only then was I able to stand face-to-face with what I needed to do to move forward. Now I know that standing in my truth means accepting my life the way it is; to rely on the answers within me and know what's right for me, despite other's opinions.

I'm not going to spend another day wishing I were thinner, prettier, have straighter teeth, longer hair, perfect feet, smaller thighs, and on and on. When I look in the mirror now, instead of seeing what I have to work on, I see how far I've come and what I like about what I see.

I'm now standing in my truth. I'm happy, despite the fact I'm not the size 10 I want to be. I'm going to wear flats because they're comfortable, not because everyone else has on heels. I'm going to encourage my family and friends to expect more out of life and go after what they want. I'm going to share my experiences that people can relate to, knowing that I'm not alone in this thing called life. With conscious control I feel empowered and victorious, like I can conquer anything. I now look forward to tomorrow, despite life's challenges.

I'm going to soak up the beauty of God's creations and enjoy the sunlight on my face. I know who I am and that gives me great inner joy, which is now showing up in my outer world. Standing in my truth feels invigorating. I feel powerful, like I can conquer the world. And there's nothing more that I can wish for you, but the same – to stand in your truth, too.

Acknowledgments

I would like to thank my Father above for putting me on the path to meet Cassandra Washington to be a part of this project. I would also like to thank my loving husband, Shawn, for giving me space to be me. Last but not least, to ALL my sisters (birth and life) who have always encouraged and believed in me. This book is dedicated to you.

Discovering a Sneaky Belief

By Allison McFadden

*"Until you make the unconscious conscious, it will direct
your life and you will call it fate."*
– C.G. Jung

I awoke to my parents' voices murmuring in the hallway as
the light flooded in under the door to my bedroom. I heard
rustling and bumping until the door opened and my dad
entered, followed by my pregnant mom. Rubbing my eyes, I
clutched my favorite stuffed animal rabbit, Bun. At that
moment, I was a sensitive and intuitive five year-old only child.

"Honey," said my dad as my mom rummaged through my
dresser behind him. "You have to wake up now and go to Kim's
house so I can take Mommy to the hospital. Your baby brother
or sister is coming."

Besides feeling groggy, I sensed my parent's tenseness. It
was around two a.m. and storming outside. My best friend
Kim's mom answered the door in her long house dress and
ushered me in. In her gentle Southern voice, she comforted me
as I settled into bed. But I sensed she too, was tense. Nervous
and anxious, it took me awhile to fall sleep. Something was
clearly wrong.

That afternoon, my dad retrieved me and took me home.
My mom and newborn baby brother were still at the hospital.
Nervous still, my tummy flipped as he pulled me onto his lap.
His crystal blue eyes, now bloodshot, welled up with tears as he
said, "Baby John was born prematurely, had complications, and
died." As my mind tried to grasp these words, his shoulders and
chest shook to stifle a sob and his hand moved up to shield his

grief from me. My insides went cold. This was the first time in my short life I saw my father cry, and it triggered a seismic rift in my world.

At the funeral I silently observed everyone and everything around me, including the tiny coffin containing Baby John – whom I never got to see – and felt alone and fearful. From that point until her death, my mother would suffer guilt and grief expressed in alcoholism.

The next summer, another tragedy befell our family. We attended a Christian camp in the Texas Hill Country so my mom could certify as a Sunday school teacher for our church. I was swimming in the pool with a little girl, playing a game of who-can-stay-under-the-water-longest-without-taking-a-breath. Distracted, I stopped playing with her for a while, then looked down into the water and saw her distorted figure at the bottom of the pool just seconds before the yelling started.

People jumped in next to me, pulling her lifeless body out of the pool to the side as another little girl started screaming and wouldn't stop. "Does anyone know CPR?" echoed out and bounced off the motel rooms around the pool where my father was inside reading. He rushed to the scene and saw the teenage lifeguard uselessly pumping her limp arms and shouted, "Move out of the way! Let me get to her!"

I climbed out of the pool and froze. In shock, I watched as my dad pumped her heart and gave her mouth-to-mouth resuscitation, stopping repeatedly to see if she breathed on her own. For what seemed like an eternity he kept on, pausing only to spit out vomit and water that came up from her lungs. Finally, he stopped, and in a leaden voice said, "She's gone. I tried, but there's no pulse." Adults helped a teenage boy pick up her lifeless body and carry her to a car as my mom arrived. Talking to witnesses about what happened, she wrapped me in a towel and held me as I sniffled and shuddered.

I was in shock. Just months ago Baby John's death was only a concept to me. This felt surreal. I was just next to her playing... and then I witnessed my dad's horrific struggle to save her... and now she's dead.

Scared and desperately wanting attention from my parents, I felt guilty. I didn't die. They didn't discuss it with me or ask how I felt. They were caught up in this new, raw grief experience. Alone, I walked amongst the trees, alternately feeling loneliness, shock, and confusion. I had no one to talk with, and it didn't feel okay to play.

A collective cloud of grief descended over the camp. At the group memorial service, the Beatle's song, "Here Comes the Sun" was played, symbolizing this tragedy and reminding my parents and me of the other. Every time it played, my dad would recall the event, sometimes choking up with regret at not saving her. We each pushed our feelings down and carried on, forever altered.

My parents were my safety and security, but now, like a rug pulled out from under me, a deep well of anxieties and fears I couldn't process, express, or articulate was uncovered. I was a sponge, absorbing their grief and emotions, but didn't know how to wring them out of me. I felt alone and abandoned without their attention, and shame and guilt for wanting it. I felt their needs were more important than mine. So, with no one to share these feelings with and no way to release them, they went deep into my subconscious, forming the "Sneaky Belief" that I don't deserve to be attended to because I don't matter.

So, in adulthood I became fearful, risk-avoidant, and lacked self-confidence. I didn't pursue an art scholarship in New York and instead attended a local university. Discounting my creative abilities, I pursued a different career path, telling myself, "I can't make a living as a starving artist."

Deep down, I felt unworthy. I split off into a "good girl" people pleaser, putting others' needs before my own, often resenting it and acting out in a passive-aggressive way. To avoid judgment and rejection, the other half, the "bad" me, became secretive, escaping into drugs and alcohol for a time. Still, I was successful in my chosen career.

At twenty-seven, my mother died suddenly of an aneurism. I wasn't coping, so a friend guided me to a therapist, where I began my journey of self-discovery. I learned that living in a state of constant high anxiety was normal for me. I uncovered family history and dynamics that had affected me for years. I dug deep and, with courage, faced up to and worked through many dysfunctions. I learned more about my inner self, and delved into alternative and spiritual interests I was passionate about. I forgave my parents and myself, yet the Sneaky Belief, hidden still, kept me from living a fully authentic life.

Soon after being honored and rewarded by my company at my 25th anniversary, management bullied me to accept a job and salary demotion, or resign without unemployment benefits. While my unhappiness there had increased, I was too afraid to risk finding something new. I had grown up there. They were like family. I was loyal and contributed to their success. But I was being pushed out, like I didn't matter. I could accept the demotion, resign with nothing, or stand and fight for a fair severance with unemployment. Suddenly, my courage rose from that deep, hidden place where the Sneaky Belief resided. The pleaser they knew wouldn't go quietly, like expected. I deserved to be attended to and I did matter! I stood firm and fought for negotiation, but they refused. I hired a lawyer and won a settlement equivalent to a fair severance including unemployment they originally denied me.

While feeling lost and searching for what to do next, two opportunities appeared simultaneously: writing this chapter and a true purpose discovery program. Both processes overlapped to reveal this Sneaky Belief from childhood, connecting the dots from my job loss to how my self worth was reflected in my job... not who I am. In the process, my Sneaky Belief was transformed to: I do matter. I am worthy of my love and I deserve to be attended to. Every day. This newfound awareness enables me to live consciously, to stand up for myself in my authentic truth, to voice my opinions, and discover what I'm really passionate about. I'm not shackled by unconscious fears and limiting beliefs, but free to pursue and live a courageous, purposeful life.

Dig deep to discover your own "Sneaky Beliefs" and you too can release yourself from what's holding you back and transform your life.

Acknowledgments

Thank you to Cassandra Washington for being my trusted life path guide; MJ Schwader for his gentle, transformational Shamanic coaching; my very talented writing buddies Anita Dixon, Elizabeth Corbell, and Johanna Rochon for their insights; my husband Scott, whose honest and constructive criticism pushed me to tie the front half to the back; and my hidden ego part Sunshine, who transformed me by revealing my suppressed memories.

Emerge

When You Hear the Call, Say "Yes"

By Darcie Beyer

"God can communicate to us through powerful feelings.
They have an energy that impels us to action. They grip
our mind and will not let us go. What is calling you?
What has the voice of God been whispering to you
through the desires of your heart? To what are you
drawn and constantly compelled to do? It could be that
God is opening the eyes of your heart to see something
that no one else is seeing, and to do something that
others aren't doing. If that is true, then move forward
and let God worry about the how."
- Tom Payne

When I was a child I had a spirit that could fill the masses
with hope and glory for the greater good. This spirit drove the
train of life with full force and plunged into lands where there
were no limitations on what one could achieve. My parents
were the driving force behind the excitement, as they told me I
could do anything if I set my mind to it. My father would ask
me, "What do you want to be when you grow up? A doctor? An
astronaut? The President of the United States?" There were no
limitations to the possibilities; only utmost favor and support in
whatever idea came out.

Then in college I had an idea that struck a different note, a
different chord that infused my father with worry and doubt.
"What if I moved to Florida, lived on the beach, and wrote a
novel?"

"Move to the beach? How would you afford food and a place to live? Why in the world would you do that after graduating college?" my father responded.

"I don't know. Maybe I'll bartend." Anything was possible if I set my mind to it, right?

No way no how was a daughter of his going to plant herself on the beach with pen and paper and nothing else to get her by. So with this reaction, believing in the insanity of it all, believing success meant making a respectable income, I closed the book and the dream. I got a job. I got another job, and another job thereafter. I learned the ropes. I learned the ins and outs of business. And eventually business turned into passion.

In 2007, I started suffering from chronic fatigue, random numbness throughout my body, and an overall feeling of life spinning out of control. After numerous tests, I was given a diagnosis of multiple sclerosis, an autoimmune disease that is recognized as untouchable, incurable, and a downward spiral. So here I was with no end in sight, no hope granted from traditional medicine, and a spirit – a gift from God – on the verge of perpetual depletion. I had just gotten married and the fear of regret from my husband plagued me. This disease could not ruin us, or the bond we shared, or the love that brought us together.

Soon after my diagnosis, my mother, a warrior of heart and soul, discovered a light at the end of the tunnel. Her fear for her daughter's disease turned into ambition and drive for a new answer, an answer not yet provided by traditional Western medicine. So in 2008 I traveled to Guatemala to spend four months with a wonderful holistic practitioner whose remedy was like no other I had ever encountered. Upon my return my symptoms of numbness and fatigue had minimalized to near nonexistence. I discovered a newfound approach to life, to food, and to appreciation for energy, health, and the people who make that possible.

I shared my healing journey with my neurologist, who replied, "That's great, but just not how we are able to treat the masses." I didn't understand. Were there obstacles? Yes. Was it a leap? Absolutely. But what if the way we knew to treat disease was a pigeon hole compared to the glorious possibilities out there to heal disease? Upon wondering, the voice of fear and reason interjected, "It's time to get back to career and life. Move on." And so I listened.

I started my own company, becoming the CEO and owner of Beyer Imaging, an office equipment company in Dallas. In seven years the company, once just a job, turned a corner into passion. I loved the people I was fortunate to meet, I loved our team, and I loved the idea of building an enterprise to serve the needs of people and places in a way that captures the essence of why it is we are here to begin with.

But even with the love of the company, the passion for health kept tugging at my core. As my health turned a corner, so did my life focus. With this focus I have met incredible healers along the way, including Jessie Lin at Metta Oriental Medicine. She taught me the beauty of mental and emotional wellbeing and how this is connected to disease. Because of her, my health and vitality has improved even more year after year.

How is this knowledge not in the hands of the masses and for the greater good of the world? I would often ponder. And the question would be overcome with all of the pressures and demands on life and how society deems it acceptable to be lived.

I gravitated toward the demands of a new home, a passageway to one day settling down in retirement and conforming to the status quo of everyday life. This status quo meant recognizing the number on a pay stub and not necessarily how it got there. The number upheld principles and values in business, yes. But it didn't signify my true calling and what I was meant to do with my newfound knowledge on the path to healing. This knowledge sat complacent at the doorstep with nobody to open the package. What about those still suffering? What about those in bitter torment because they cannot function like their God-given true selves? But who am I to share this knowledge and who are they to listen? What if nobody believes me?

"You are ready for this journey and mission," I heard God whisper. "It is yours to have and to hold. Do you say yes?"

Who was I to say no? But I had built a beautiful company with a team I admired for their faith, patience, and workmanship. And if I walked away from this industry I know and love would people call me insane? And would this name-calling instigate a fear to make me go back? I wanted nothing but great things for my team and felt I needed to protect them from the unknown. Letting go of this drove a stake through my heart, but who was I to say no?

"Let go of the reigns," came another whisper. "Place your company in the hands of another suitor." This voice I trusted. This voice I trusted more than the feelings of doubt and uncertainty for what lay ahead. And with this voice I decided to trust my company to another leader in order to pursue the original message of my father – anything is possible if you set your mind to it.

The search for the suitor unveiled many potential offers, to some of which I said no, but one special leader to whom I said yes. This leader I trust with my whole being. Because of this pursuit, I see a vision for the company bigger than anything I could have done on my own. My team and my clients are in wonderful hands.

Now it's time for me to put my attention toward improved health throughout the world. I don't have a clear roadmap in hand that will lead me from point A to point B and all other points beyond. I don't know how this unfolds, but I do know this: I've opened my heart to my true calling and the book is ready to be written. I will plunge into this journey with no map to get me through other than the faith that has brought me here today as good as new. This faith will lead this venture to the next level of engagement, now that I have said, "Yes."

Acknowledgments

To my dear friend Cassandra, thank you for the inspiration to write with you, and for opening the doors to another world of acknowledgment and knowingness from within.

Emerge

A Leap of Faith

By Kali Rodriguez

"Our deepest fear is not that we are inadequate. Our deepest fear is that we are powerful beyond measure. It is our light, not our darkness that most frightens us. We ask ourselves, 'Who am I to be brilliant, gorgeous, talented, fabulous?' Actually, who are you not to be? You are a child of God. Your playing small does not serve the world. There is nothing enlightened about shrinking so that other people won't feel insecure around you. We are all meant to shine, as children do. We were born to make manifest the glory of God that is within us. It's not just in some of us; it's in everyone. And as we let our own light shine, we unconsciously give other people permission to do the same. As we are liberated from our own fear, our presence automatically liberates others."
– Marianne Williamson

Looking out my hotel room window on a hot August afternoon in Las Vegas, I could almost feel the heat through the glass pane. I planned to touch up a few documents to print and then leave for client meetings. As I sat at my laptop and began to type, my hands began to tremble.

Twice I stood up and walked around, deep breathing from years of yoga training, and sat back down. Each time I raised my hands over the keyboard, they were shaking. My legs felt weak and shaky too, my breath short and difficult. I kept telling myself, "This will go away. I'm healthy and strong." But in that moment I felt sick and weak.

That day wasn't the last of shaking legs and anxiety. Over the next month, along with other symptoms I had thought were random – exhaustion, cramping hands, feet tingling and numb, and muscle pain – I began to realize that something was clearly not right. My diet was better than most, I exercised and did yoga, I stayed away from processed and fast food, and I cleansed and detoxed. How was I sick?

Thank goodness I found a functional medicine doctor. His knowledge and approach resonated with my 20-year passion for holistic healing. We embarked on a journey to heal thyroid and adrenal issues, low blood sugar, low iron and vitamin D, and food allergies.

At first I felt better. Yet a year later, many symptoms and the anxiety persisted, and new ones had appeared. My doctor kept saying there was something else.

One day, as I lay on his table overwhelmed with anxiety, he revealed an energetic block related to my job. I confessed that I hadn't wanted to take it, but felt like I had to for financial reasons. I had wanted to own a wellness center for 20 years, and somehow never pursued it.

I knew that I wanted more, had a passion in my heart, and had gifts to share. But in my mind, leaving my career wasn't an option. We needed my income. I felt trapped, and deep down I was scared. My career was stressful, with long hours and travel, but I was afraid to leave. It wasn't a life I wanted, but it was the life I knew. And what we know is comfortable, even if it is miserable.

My doctor explained that sometimes it takes getting sick for someone to make changes, and said the world needs more people like me. As I lay there with tears streaming down my face, he said something I will always remember: "Do what you love and the money will come."

I didn't know how that was possible, but I asked God and the Universe to please send it to me.

I began reading *The Secret* for the fourth time. Within months, I started a network marketing business. Although I had tried MLM many times with no success, I saw an opportunity to have the life of health and freedom I desperately wanted. Nine months later, I was laid off. Although financially scary, I welcomed the opportunity to focus on my health, my business, and plan my upcoming wedding. My fiancé Kris and I climbed to the top of Mt. Bonnell overlooking the Austin skyline, set goals, and began creating a life by design.

We attended trainings and listened to every personal development audio we could. I was becoming more skilled, yet the resulting money still wasn't there. Some days my efforts were sporadic and all I could hear were the "no's". But it didn't stop me. I continued to affirm the life I want to live.

That summer, we went to a seminar to develop the mindset of a millionaire. When it came time to purchase their program, Kris wanted to buy; I didn't. What they said resonated with me, but I wouldn't take on more debt, even if it might change my life.

Kris looked me in the eye as we sat in the courtyard with the sun beating down, and called me out: "Do you not have any faith?" *Of course I do*, I thought to myself. But in that moment, I couldn't feel it; in fact, I could feel its absence.

They had us do an exercise to symbolically break through our fears. Mine was financial instability. It had fueled my decisions for too many years. I was never willing to follow my heart because I saw financial risk in leaving my income. In the exercise, we were to break a wooden arrow that was against our throat. I hesitated, my arrow broke unevenly, and I ended up with a cut across my chest. They said all weekend, "how you do anything is how you do everything" and I realized it was how I did everything. I hesitated all the time. I didn't trust myself, and I didn't trust my decisions.

I named it "The Hesitation Scar" and left wanting to learn from this breakthrough. For months I reflected on my life. Where did my hesitancy come from and how could I change it? I was seeking the answer and found it at a Bob Proctor conference. His teachings on the mind revealed the answer I sought. I understood my choices, my lack of success in network marketing, why I had been sick, and why I stayed stuck for so many years in a life that looked great on the outside, but that on the inside felt like I was dying a little bit each year.

I learned that doubt, worry, and fear manifested as anxiety, and suppressed anxiety led to dis-ease. My body was not at ease. And I learned that when you have faith – not blind faith, but faith from understanding – fear can't coexist. Both fear and faith are invisible, and with both, you choose to believe something you cannot see.

That weekend I had the opportunity to partner with the Proctor Gallagher Institute. I saw the future I imagined for myself and the ability to help others create a life they desire. In that moment, I could feel fear knocking at the door, my heart pounding and hands sweating. My past was trying to keep me comfortable while my future was pulling me forward. Kris was cheering me on. This was my chance to choose faith. So I did.

I took an exhilarating leap of faith that day, with no hesitation. I had no idea how it would happen. I just knew it was the right step because it gave me life and lifted me up.

I used this new education, continuing to dig deep into the garden of my mind, to unearth the limiting beliefs that held me back. I saw a 4 year-old girl who accidentally pushed her sister off a chair, and learned not to push for what you want because someone could get hurt. I saw the teenager who desperately wanted acceptance, and learned to follow the crowd. I saw the young college woman who – just when she was starting to come into her own – was raped, and feeling overpowered, couldn't find her voice to scream and fight back. I saw the successful corporate workaholic, striving for achievement, yet devoid of passion and fulfillment. I identified the fears: of rejection, of not being liked or accepted, of expressing myself, and the fear of stepping out because I believed no one would follow me. I saw a woman with a passion in her heart for wellness, but had defined herself as sick for years.

So many people suppress the real expression inside, living in fear, and numb to the possibility of a life they love. We are programmed to live that way, but we can choose differently. Our choices lead us to a life that is silent desperation, emptiness, and regret, or inspired, purposeful, and fulfilled.

This choice for me was to create my life, to stand up for myself and what I believe, to speak my truth, and to lead with my heart. I rub my hesitation scar, gently remind myself the fear is there to protect me, and then choose faith; faith in myself, my abilities, and my capacity to share and inspire. And instead of dying inside a little each year, I can feel myself coming alive more with each passing month.

With each step forward, my vision and desire to make a difference in the world grows. My vision is to empower people to live a life of healing, health, wisdom, and wealth. I believe that living a life you love is an integral part of a well life. For me to fulfill my vision of empowering others to live in wellness, I had to go through my own path to healing. I had to believe I could make a difference in one life – mine – before I could for others on a bigger scale. I am here to help people be W.E.L.L. – to Wakeup Everyday Loving Life.

Acknowledgments

With deep gratitude, I'd like to acknowledge our program coach Cassandra Washington for who she is, and for her being gentle, encouraging, and oh-so patient with me through this process. To my amazing husband and hero Kris: You are my best friend, my rock, and my heart. Your courage inspires me every day and your support strengthens me. I love our life and I love you.

Conclusion: Learn, Connect, and Soar!

"I can do things you cannot, you can do things I cannot; together we can do great things." – Mother Teresa

The authors of this book are not the same people they were before we started this project. Here's what some of them had to say:

*"**Transform Through Writing** is a great course. I figured the transformation would come through how I was writing, not necessarily on how I would transform while writing. This came at the right time for me – still in the grieving process, yet wanting to move forward, but just treading water not knowing how to move on.*

I have always loved to journal and write and would spend hours upon hours some days, only to feel like I'd wasted the day away. But then I realized it wasn't a waste, but an opportunity to share life lessons with others. I was like a kid in the candy store, going from one lesson to the next. I was amazed at how relaxed I felt on the coaching calls – no hesitancy at all to speak freely, while other business calls left me anxious and nervous-sounding. I knew this was meant to be. This was my opportunity to write and learn more about where I have been and where the road might take me.

Both Cassandra and MJ made you feel like an instant friend – very caring toward others. I felt very comfortable in talking with them, even while they were breaking down my walls and I found myself in tears (good tears!). They helped me transform and become more confident in myself. I am so thankful to have this opportunity to become a published author in this book – it's truly a dream come true."

~ Susan W. Corbran

"Before I joined this program, I had been searching and struggling for a long time to find my purpose. I had spent significant funds on other programs, but to no avail. I had met Cassandra at an Ambitious women's conference in 2014. God brought our paths back together in 2015, where her break-out session stirred up something in me that caused me to take immediate action and jump in with both feet. When we began this journey, I was expecting it to be all laugh-out-loud fun. However, I wasn't prepared for the outcome. I never expected this program would take me down into the crevasses of my soul and bring me out again, transformed and excited about the possibilities that life now has to offer. I can never thank God enough for putting Cassandra and MJ in my life. You have been blessed with an awesome gift that allows people a safe place to grow and transform. Your sense of discernment "draws" out of a person more than they thought they could be, even though it is tough and painful at times. Thank you Cassandra and MJ, for helping me find my voice. Yes YES!"   **~ Suzanne R. Duque**

"This experience was amazing and wonderful. Before I started this program, I was not sure if I was going to be able to write because of my limiting belief – that I didn't have money. But that was not true. Cassandra and MJ made it easy and set up a payment plan for this program. It was the best investment I made for myself this year. I had some reservations during this process, fears that I addressed to my family, Cassandra and MJ, and my writing community. I was not alone in this journey of self-awareness. I saw the concerns disappear one by one and I became more confident and relaxed with my writing. I would recommend this program to my friends to help then untangle, challenge their limiting beliefs, and awaken the creative parts in their life."   **~ Sandra Brooks**

*"Having written a chapter for last year's book, I jumped at the chance to be involved again because the experience helped me transform a life upheaval I had recently experienced. I was, however, afraid of staying in my own head when expressing my feelings, which was my tendency. For this book, I wanted to really grow and dig deep so that my chapter would be more impactful for the reader than I felt my first one was. At the same time the **Transform Through Writing** program came up, Cassandra was also leading a **Discover Your True Purpose Program**, which I also joined. Both programs worked in synchronicity to help me evolve. I didn't just dig deeply; I journeyed to the hidden parts of my psyche to reveal early childhood wounds and limiting beliefs that had controlled me. I thought MJ as a writing coach was going to be highly critical. I could not have been more wrong! Like Cassandra, MJ is a nurturing, soul-centered person whose purpose is to help us unblock and reveal the voice of our soul through the honest expression of transformative writing. Safely supported by Cassandra, MJ, and my amazing writing buddies in the program, I learned techniques that unblocked me so I could unleash my "Inner Cracken," decimating my fears of writing. I can't wait to be a part of the next book!"*   *~ **Allison McFadden***

"This is the second book I've co-written with Cassandra and MJ. The first book required me to reach deep within my life for experiences that I would not normally have shared with anyone. In so doing, I found it had a dramatic impact on me. This time, I was challenged again when I found out the theme was "Stand in Your Truth". I immediately knew I had to write about my personal life story regarding my trials and tribulations of living an alternative lifestyle. I initially had the fear of being vulnerable and revealing my personal story. However, what I learned after writing the first book is that my writing made a difference to several people. They related to my story and it helped them.

Making a difference in their lives was worth it to me. In this book I realize others have struggled as I have. I'm willing to risk my fear if I can make a difference to someone again. I've learned that it doesn't matter what people think of you; it's what you think about yourself that is important in life. I want to thank Cassandra for allowing me to share my story in this book. Cassandra and MJ are awesome coaches and trainers and provided excellent guidance during our book-writing journey. I'm thrilled and honored to be able to co-write another book with them again."

~ *Ilda Grimaldo*

"My biggest fear before joining the program was becoming part of a very vulnerable and transparent community of writers. I never had problems writing intimate feelings and life details for my eyes only, but I was challenged to trust at another level with every writing exercise I submitted during the program. My favorite part of the program was when I discovered that a greater depth of writing and self-discovery comes when I become vulnerable, transparent, and use streams of consciousness to express myself. If I were to recommend this program to my best friend, I would tell them to dive in, be challenged, be set free, and be transformed through writing. It is more than just a project; it is an experience."

~ *Anita Boutwell-Dixon*

*"By being a part of **Transform Through Writing** I have transformed. I had always dreamed of becoming a writer, but always had doubt, or thought that I didn't have time. However, this opportunity has made a dream become a reality. Because of all the support and tips, I know how to eliminate any preconceived writing obstacles. I am now pushing myself to grow even further by publishing a novel! The support from this group has been phenomenal! Cassandra has been a great mentor to me over the past few years. She gives of herself*

unselfishly and has such a nurturing soul. MJ also provides very insightful feedback and has the gift to translate ways to get you to write from your soul in such a powerful manner. I loved how this program took us on a journey! Through weekly writing assignments, we were being prepped to dig deeper for our final chapters. We were also able to connect with writing buddies to help us grow with give and take feedback, and at the same time establish lasting relationships. If anyone has dreams that they think are unattainable, obstacles that they can't get over, or just burdens of life, then this is the right program, because transformation is guaranteed to occur." **~ Johanna Rochon**

"I highly recommend this program to anyone who will listen to that inner voice that calls you to fulfill your purpose in life.

I want to give thanks to God for putting Cassandra Washington on my path. The day I met Cassandra was a divine appointment; with her ministry she helped me reconnect with the wish of my childhood to write a book. My challenges were time and my financial situation at that moment. However, I decided to take the challenge in faith, and I have no regrets. Through the process I understood God's revelation in my life: To fulfill God's purpose and be a blessing by writing and sharing my story with the world. I now see and understand that each of the writers and readers are fulfilling a cycle and purpose for which God has called us into this season. We are a chapter in each other's lives.

I also want to thank MJ for sharing his experience with every one of us, for all of his advice, for helping us to be better writers, and for showing us how to polish the rough edges in the writing to bring out the best in our stories.

'Therefore encourage one another and build each other up, just as in fact you are doing.' 1Thes 5:11

I look forward to having the opportunity to continue writing, and in the process, to continue to refine me."

~ Maria J. Martinez

"I had written in my goals that I wanted to write a book, or be a part of one... at the very least, learn how to write. I met Cassandra a year after I had been diagnosed with breast cancer and I knew when I was in her training class that day that I was meant to join this book.

She showed me that there was a way that I could not only share my story, but to learn to write at the same time. Cassandra pushed me, in the gentlest way, to have me really dig deep, to be vulnerable and open up. I appreciate all of her support and genuine care in the entire process.

MJ was amazing to work with. In our work together, he pointed out another direction that I should write about, which truly helped my message. He also encouraged me to pursue speaking, and for that I am truly thankful.

Working with both Cassandra and MJ was inspirational and transformational. I feel blessed to be a part of this book along with so many amazing authors and women. If you are looking to grow yourself, to really dig deep and transform on the inside, this is the program for you. Thank you so much Cassandra and MJ. I'm looking forward to working with you both again one day!"
~ Michelle J. Perzan

"When I first started this writing process I was apprehensive. I could not decide if I should tell my truth. My writing gurus, MJ Schwader and Cassandra Washington shared their encouragement and wise counsel with me every step of the way. I am so appreciative of being a member of this writing community."
~ Patricia Alston-Roshon

"My biggest fear when I started writing this book was that I would not have enough time to do it. To my surprise, I was able to find time. I feel so blessed to have met Cassandra

Washington at Ambitious Women Conference. I have wanted to write a book and this is a dream come true. Thank you to Cassandra Washington and MJ for all the love, support, and guidance you have given to me. Without your help, this would not be possible. I also want to thank God for making this happen. I would love to write more in the future, and now I know who to seek for help and guidance. I highly recommend Cassandra Washington and MJ Schwader as coach and trainer."
~ Precilla Feliciano Calara

"Transformation is never easy. I hope this book gives hope and courage to others to attempt to become butterflies instead of remaining caterpillars. I want to thank Cassandra Washington and MJ Schwader for giving me the opportunity to become part of this project. It has been a blessing."
~ Elizabeth Corbell

"To Cassandra and MJ, thank you for this writing experience. You bring thought-provoking ideas to engage the hearts and souls of many. Thank you for sharing your gifts with my fellow co-authors and me." **~ Darcie Beyer**

"I had never written before, but enjoy other people's writing and stories. When the opportunity appeared in my life to be a part of this project, I had many reservations. But my husband said, 'Go Squirrely go; it will be a fun learning experience.' Always wanting to have fun, I embraced my new adventure, and haven't doubted it for a second. I enjoyed the amazing guidance Cassandra and MJ offered, while learning and being a part of this amazing group of women. I had so much fun, and would encourage everyone who has ever dreamed of writing their own story to be a part of Cassandra's group. I am so thankful for all the gifts this process has brought into my life." **~ Diana Towsley**

"Before joining the **Transform Through Writing** program, I believed I had a story and a message inside, but didn't know how to express it. I also felt like the challenges and transformation I went through weren't as significant as the powerful stories of others who had experienced major life obstacles. Working with a group helped me to realize we all have a story and a message, and as with each individual, all of them are unique and inspiring. Through the coaching process, Cassandra listened closely for and guided me to the expression of my unique message. The stream of conscious writing process itself was my favorite part, as it is truly healing to release thoughts and feelings that have been suppressed for so long. I would tell my best friend and anyone, 'Just do it. Your story, your message, they are valuable gifts to give the world.'"

~ Kali Rodriguez

The authors have been turbocharged by the experience. So will you! You will be inspired and recharged by the forward movement and progress of the group, and you are less likely to stall out. You will experience greater clarity and grow more confident knowing you always have a place to find the answers you seek. You will become comfortable with uncertainty and trust yourself more. You will witness yourself taking bigger risks in the safety net of community. It starts with a one degree shift!

Why don't you join us? Connect with One Degree Shift community at www.onedegreeshift.com.

Meet Cassandra

Colleagues and scholars describe her as an... ARCHITECT, TEACHER, ACHIEVER, STIMULATOR, RELATOR, LEARNER, but for Cassandra the one word that describes her most is LOVE. As she explains it, "Love is the reason I do what I do. I see the difference YOU make, and I feel compelled to be a part of it. If I support you to fulfill your higher purpose and you go on to support someone else, I, in turn, fulfill my mission to transform the world one person at a time. That's love!" ❤

A seasoned coach, gifted communicator, and trainer, Cassandra is a Licensed True Purpose® Coach and Certified Dream Coach® who motivates her clients to take heart-inspired action toward their goals. She coaches clients privately, in small groups, and leads a thriving virtual community of difference makers. Cassandra is skilled at helping you learn how to connect and trust your inner guidance, clear blocks, discover your deeper purpose, navigate the turbulence of uncertainty, and manifest your difference.

Cassandra works with leaders and messengers to sharpen their message and be more powerful communicators so they can reach more people and have greater impact. Whether it is creating new content or repurposing an existing message, she is committed to helping leaders speak from their heart in a way that produces results. Her professional development firm, Exceed Learning, works with organizations to develop world-class content and corporate training programs that promote engagement, contribution, collaboration, and bottom-line results.

For Cassandra, powerful communication means speaking from the heart, and it is her pivotal life lesson. And, perhaps her deeper work is really about redefining power.

She felt called to be a powerful, stable pillar of strength for her family at an early age. After two traumatic events in middle school – the loss of her favorite cousin to a tragic car accident and her parents' ugly divorce – Cassandra made a decision to abandon her tears and her softness. She became a workhorse who mastered the ability to keep situations under control and her emotions tightly guarded.

Through her own journey of personal development and transformation, she had several epiphany moments that set her on a path of purpose. And now she realizes how to integrate the power of vulnerability, uncertainty, and an open heart.

Cassandra is the author of a top-selling business skills book, *How to Manage Unacceptable Employee Behavior*, and she is featured in leadership expert John Maxwell's book, *Everyone Communicates, Few Connect*, and is co-author in One Degree Shift's Amazon best-seller, *Strengthen Your Wings*. She's a sought-after speaker and "go-to" trainer with a list of satisfied clients that extends across North America and internationally.

When she's not coaching or training, she enjoys the beach, lazy weekends watching marathon makeover TV shows while snacking on Flammin' Hot Cheetos, or spending time with valued friends and relatives.

Cassandra has coached countless men and women to push their limits and realize their greatest potential. And, now she's ready to motivate you.

Visit Cassandra at www.CassandraWashington.com or connect with her on Facebook or Twitter. She would love to hear from you!

Meet MJ Schwader

Using humor, a strong intuition, and a lifetime of experience, published author and writing coach MJ Schwader guides coaches, speakers, healers, and conscious entrepreneurs to craft and promote their writing, from concept to the marketplace.

MJ holds a degree from Oregon State University in Technical Journalism with an emphasis in Business Management. After working for several years as a technical writer contracting to high tech companies in the United States and Pacific Rim countries, MJ created and operated a restaurant for five years before becoming a Life and Business Coach to other coaches and speakers.

When business and life coaching clients learned of MJ's experience in writing and publishing, they asked him to help them publish their books. As a result, MJ founded the collaborative 10-book series, *A Guide to Getting It*, with each book filled with chapters written by Life and Business Coaches to highlight principles and ideas supported in the coaching process.

Following the *Guide* series, MJ partnered with Equine Facilitated Learning and Coaching trainer Kathy Pike to publish two collaborative books in the *Horse as Teacher* book series. Equine Facilitated Learning and Coaching is a method of using horses as guides to personal and business development work.

In 2014, MJ helped Cassandra Washington publish *Strengthen Your Wings: Amazing Stories for the Journey*, the first collaborative book in a series published by Cassandra's community, One Degree Shift. In 2015, the two teamed up again to develop *Transform Through Writing*, a writing program designed to help authors of the second book in the series,

Emerge: True Stories of Courage and Truth, create powerful transformational chapters.

Weaving ancient principles of energy consciousness learned in 15 years of shamanic training with nearly 20 years of experience as a writing coach and internet marketer, MJ helps clients shift their awareness, ignite their inspiration, and clear beliefs that are holding them back from achieving success. Having worked with over 200 published authors, MJ has developed a profound and successful process for breaking through limited thinking and fears to help clients remove blocks and create transformational writing. In the process, the clients are also transformed.

MJ learned writing coaching techniques from 30 years of experience in the publishing industry, as well as training at Coach University. One of the first 5000 coaches in the world, MJ has been a pioneer in coaching writers.

To contact MJ, visit www.inspiredlifepublications.com or email MJ@inspiredlifepublications.com.

Contributing Authors

Patricia Alston-Rochon received a B.A., M.Ed., and a Master's in Educational Administration and Leadership, then worked as a school administrator and hearing officer. A mother and a grandmother, she currently resides in Texas. Patricia can be reached at palsroc@yahoo.com.

Darcie Beyer is a wife and mother to two beautiful boys, James and Beau. She climbed the business ladder, only to find what she truly wants was not at the top. She delves in goodness and wholeheartedness and wishes to share her experience with the world of healing through turbulent waters. She can be reached at darciebeyer@gmail.com.

Anita Boutwell-Dixon is a minister of the Gospel, entrepreneur, and an Air Force veteran. She holds a degree in Human Resource Management and a certificate of Biblical Counseling from Midwest Bible College. She has held several leadership positions in her local church and has a passion to see the broken-hearted made whole and set free from depression. She recently retired from the corporate world and launched her own company, Executive Order LLC. This was a direct result of being transformed through this writing project. While in the military, she lived in several states and England, and now resides in Racine, WI. She believes that a merry heart is like medicine, and she is intentional about finding at least one reason daily to have a good belly laugh. Anita is available for speaking engagements and can be reached at Preachingirl@minister.com.

Sandra Brooks is a professional face painter who enjoys making smiles her canvas. As a Young Living essential oil distributer, she loves engaging with others and sharing its benefits. After a career as a dedicated wife and mother, Sandra is an empty nester who now stays busy investing in her personal growth and redirecting her heart and mind to new passions where she can continue to serve others. An avid movie-goer, Sandra looks forward to writing more, perhaps taking a crack at romance novels. Sandra resides in Cedar Hill, TX and is married, with two adult children and one adoring grandson. Email Sandra at sandrabrooks250@gmail.com or connect with her on Facebook.

Precilla Feliciano Calara was born in the Philippines and came to the United States to experience the American Dream. She received a Bachelor of Science Degree in Civil Engineering, and then became a Real Estate Broker and Investor, as well as an Executive Consultant with Ambit Energy, the first in the Rio Grande Valley. She won the Ambit Energy Perseverance Award in 2009. Precilla believes that America is the "dream land" where every person is blessed to have an equal opportunity to achieve success and prosperity through hard work, determination, and initiative. She lives in Harlingen, Texas. For speaking engagements, contact Precilla at 956-535-2187 or visit www.PrecillaCalara.com.

Elizabeth Corbell is the Office Services Administrator for Silverleaf Resorts, where she has worked for the past 19 years. Her latest transformation has been to finally lose weight! With the help of her personal trainer, Danny Fuentes, she has lost 65 pounds in less than a year. She has been married to Sonny for 32 years and has three wonderful children, Alvin, Crystal, and Chloe. Elizabeth is a vibrant Christian whose life revolves around her family, the gym, and her job. For more information or to contact Elizabeth, email Corbell7777@gmail.com.

Susan W. Corbran received a B.A. in Elementary Education, then chose to be a stay-at-home mom. She has worked at various times as a substitute teacher, the director of children's ministry, delivering flowers, and working in home-based businesses. She is currently an independent consultant with Ambit Energy. After experiencing the death of her husband to cancer, Sue's dream is to start a ministry for those who have lost a loved one and are dealing with grief, sending out T.O.Y. (Thinking of You) bags with inspirational quotes, a handkerchief (because tissues run out), and other comforting items. Her goal is to publish her life stories, as well as write fictional stories for children. Sue volunteers to teach Bible lessons to K-5th graders at her church, and loves to write, travel, golf, and read. She lives in Meadville, PA. You can read some of her stories at www.suecobran.com.

Suzanne R. Duque and her husband Johnny are professional network marketers with Ambit Energy, where they enjoy helping people dream again and make a difference in their lives. Suzanne's middle son died in a car accident in 1996 at the age of 16, impacting her life in ways she is still learning from. She has two living sons and three grandchildren. She lives in West Columbia, TX where she and Johnny live on twenty-five acres. You can usually find her barefooted, feeding the deer, playing with horses, spoiling her dog, or nurturing some small animal. Suzanne is currently working on another book that will be published next year. She is available for speaking engagements. Visit her website, www.suzanneduque.com for more information.

Johnnene Gay used to live her life by osmosis – if she waited around long enough something might soak in and her life might change. Now, her motto is "Just Do It!" She is an Independent Senior Consultant in Ambit Energy, an energy company in a $500 billion industry. Her goal is to partner with serious, business-minded people to create the life of their dreams – and hers. Johnnene lives with her loving and supportive husband Shawn and two active sons, Julian and Stephan, in Plano, Texas. She loves to write and read self-help books, motivational materials, and most important, The Bible. She can be reached through her business website: www.johnnene.energy526.com or email at jag.hurry@gmail.com.

Ilda Grimaldo helps people pursue their personal goals and aspirations by building a residual income on a part-time basis in the emerging energy deregulation industry as an Ambit Energy entrepreneur. She is also a Stress Intervention Specialist, Tong Ren Energy Practitioner, and owner of A Positive Touch Massage Therapy, promoting acutherapy, energy healing, and therapeutic massage. Ilda was a contributing author in *Strengthen Your Wings: Amazing Stories for the Journey*, a best seller in the Amazon self-help motivational category. Ilda inspires and motivates her family, colleagues, and friends with her passion for helping the people around her. She lives in San Antonio, TX. For more information, call 210-508-7314 or visit www.ilda.whyambitworks.com.

Maria J. Martinez is a Parent Liaison in Irving Texas, and a marketing consultant with Ambit Energy. Her work allows her to fulfill God's purpose in her life, providing a blessing for parents, volunteers, mentors, students, teachers, and staff by engaging community in her workplace. Maria is a woman of faith and prayer. To contact her, email duquesa1212@yahoo.com.

Allison McFadden has always followed her intuition as she studied art in high school and college, went on to be a Commercial Broadcast Producer, then Creative Business Manager, and finally as a Recruiter and HR Generalist prior to leaving the Advertising/Marketing/PR agency she'd been with for 25 years. She is re-discovering her essence, blessing, and mission in life, and is pursuing a new purpose-oriented career of service. She happily lives life "in the flow" with her husband Scott McFadden and two orange Tabby Main Coon cat brothers, Barney and Brewster in Dallas, Texas. She records and edits her own voice in a converted closet studio for commercials, eLearning, industrials, characters, and more. Demos and contact information are on www.allisonmcfadden.com.

Michelle Perzan is a self-employed, stay-at-home mom with a part-time energy business, where she helps people save money. Her passion is to help and encourage other people who are struggling in life to see that their faith, patience, and attitude are powerful tools. Michelle is happily married to the love of her life Aaron, and has three wonderful boys, Daniel, David, and Dylan. A Canadian native, she has lived in Texas for nine years and has made it home. Her goal is to become a speaker, sharing her story in hopes of motivating and inspiring others who are experiencing difficulty in their life. You can reach Michelle at michelle@mperzan.com or at www.michelleperzan.com.

Johanna Rochon has always dreamed of becoming a writer. This publication has helped propel her in fulfilling that dream. She has had several years experience as a Project Manager in the Financial Services Industry, after graduating from Texas Woman's University with a B.B.A in Human Resources and a M.B.A. She is also an alumni of the INROADS organization. Johanna's passions are writing, entrepreneurship, listening to live music, and mentoring. She currently resides in Dallas, TX and is working on her first novel and furthering her career as a writer. Johanna can be contacted at johannarochon@yahoo.com.

Kali Rodriguez is an entrepreneur, author, speaker, activist, wellness advocate, facilitator, and coach. After a 13-year career in Corporate America, Kali listened to her heart and took a leap of faith into entrepreneurship. She partnered with the Proctor Gallagher Institute to become a Certified Facilitator for the powerful transformational program, *Thinking Into Results.* Acting on a 20-year passion for holistic health and wellness, she completed certification as an Integrative Nutrition Health Coach. In 2015, Kali founded Think Health Think Wealth LLC, with a vision to empower individuals and companies to achieve their highest potential of wellness, success, fulfillment, and freedom. Kali loves reading, yoga, healthy living, Marching Against Monsanto, and Texas Longhorn Football. She lives in Austin, Texas with her amazing husband Kris, and their adorable pup Allie. Connect with Kali Rodriguez via email at Kali@ThinkHealthThinkWealth.com, visit her website at www.ThinkHealthThinkWealth.com, or check out her business page at Facebook.com/ThinkHealthThinkWealth.

Gillian Smith is a teacher, preacher, consultant, author, and humanitarian. She became an international licensed Minister in 1997, and in 1999 traveled to Jersey City to work with local churches, in which she was a pioneer of a type of liturgical dance that included sign language within the choreography. She traveled coast-to-coast building churches and doing the work of Kingdom Building. In 2000, Gillian established Haven International Ministries, which has been recognized by non-profit organizations across the country for the work they do in their communities. For speaking engagements, call 424-757-8596 or email powerleadersall@gmail.com.

Diana Towsley is a mom, a wife, a daughter, a sister, and a friend. She's predominantly worked in the worlds of advertising and non-profits. She loves being outside. You may catch her busting a move to a Beyoncé song, thinking she can leap small buildings. Diana is most happy when she's of service to others, encouraging and supporting them to see their greatness. Reach out to Diana at dktowsley@hotmail.com.